What Color Is Your Personality?

Red, Orange, Yellow, Green . . .

Carol Ritberger, Ph.D.

HAY HOUSE, INC. • Carlsbad, California • New York City • London
Sydney • Johannesburg • Vancouver • Hong Kong • New Delhi

LIFE Styles

Copyright © 2000 by Carol Ritberger

Published and distributed in the United States by: Hay House, Inc.: www.hayhouse.com •
Published and distributed in Australia by: Hay House Australia Pty. Ltd.: www.hayhouse.com.au • *Published and distributed in the United Kingdom by:* Hay House UK, Ltd.: www.hayhouse.co.uk • *Published and distributed in the Republic of South Africa by:* Hay House SA (Pty), Ltd.: www.hayhouse.co.za • *Distributed in Canada by:* Raincoast: www.raincoast.com • *Published in India by:* Hay House Publishers India: www.hayhouse.co.in

Editorial: Jill Kramer • *Design:* Christy Salinas • *Illustrations:* Vivienne Flesher

Library of Congress Cataloging-in-Publication Data

Ritberger, Carol.
     What color is your personality? :   red, orange, yellow, green— /
Carol Ritberger.
      p.   cm.
    ISBN 1-56170-651-5 (hardcover) • ISBN 978-1-4019-2414-0 (tradepaper)
    1. Typology (Psychology)   2. Color—Psychological aspects.
3. Chakras.   I. Title.
BF698.3.R58   1999
155.2'64—dc21
                                              99-12898
                                               CIP

[Material based on *Your Personality, Your Health* © 1998 by Carol Ritberger, Ph.D.]

ISBN 978-1-4019-2414-0

15 14 13 12   8 7 6 5
1st Printing, December 1999
5th Printing, October 2012

Printed in USA

Contents

Introduction 5

Chapter 1:   Personality: It's in Your Genes..................13
Chapter 2:   Color and Personality................................39
Chapter 3:   What Color Is Your Personality? 55
             • The Personality Color Indicator 59
Chapter 4:   The Red Personality 71
Chapter 5:   The Orange Personality 87
Chapter 6:   The Yellow Personality 103
Chapter 7:   The Green Personality 119
Chapter 8:   The Role of Personality in Illness 135

About the Author 167

Introduction

Have you ever wondered why you instinctively do things? Have you ever noticed how some people are easier to get along with than others? Have you ever asked yourself why it is that when you get stressed, the stress seems to show up in the same place in your body every time?

What is it that makes us different? It is this basic question that has motivated physicians, thinkers, and healers to explore human nature to better understand why we act and think the way we do. Personally, it is that question that has driven me to become an avid student of human behavior and has led to 18 years of researching how personality, stress, and emotions contribute to the formation of disease in the human body.

So, what really is the difference maker? *It is personality*. When you think about personality, think of it as your automatic pilot. It creates the involuntary behavioral patterns necessary for you to function and to survive, and represents both your inner genetic coding and the outward direction you will take in life. Your personality is the organizing principle that affects all aspects of your life: your lifestyle, your work habits, your relationships, your stress responses, and your health.

Personality represents the orderly arrangement of attitudes, beliefs, thoughts, emotional reactions, and coping mechanisms that help you deal with life. Your personality is what establishes the boundaries through which you live your life. If life complements your personality boundaries, then you will feel a sense of control over your destiny, and you feel happy. However, if life's challenges force you to move outside of your personality boundaries, then you experience stress and emotional discomfort and view life from a negative perspective.

Your personality has two aspects: traits and characteristics. Traits are the result of inherent genetic coding that determines the way your brain develops and functions around mental processing, which is how you gather and process information and make decisions.

There are four distinctive personality information/ processing styles that are categorized in this book: RED, ORANGE, YELLOW, and GREEN. Since traits are genetic, how you choose to express your personality uniqueness will be fully determined by the time you reach age 13, and then you will find yourself living your life in a distinctive way that complements your personality boundaries for the remainder of your years. Traits are the part of personality that you cannot change, and the truth is, you don't want to, because it is your traits that determine your personality strengths and your natural talents.

The second aspect of personality is characteristics. Characteristics are the behavioral patterns that you develop as a result of what you have learned. They reflect your biographical history and cultural influences, and determine how your environment is impacting you.

Characteristics are responsible for the formation of your learned habits, your comfort zones, and the idiosyncratic patterns of behavior you create over the course of your lifetime. As you grow and change in life due to the demands of your environment, what you are actually changing are your personality characteristics. Characteristics are the flexible parts of personality that allow you to adapt and survive. However, what determines your level of flexibility and to what extent you change, is driven by the boundaries predetermined by your personality traits.

When you combine traits and characteristics, you get a composite picture of personality type. Every personality type— RED, ORANGE, YELLOW and GREEN—has its own set of strengths and weaknesses. Here is where relationships play a key role in the development of your personality characteristics. If your relationships support your personality type and allow you to work from your strengths, then you will build characteristics around a strong sense of self, you will display self-confidence, and you will have a positive sense of self-worth. However, if your relationships are difficult and the differences between you and others create self-worth struggles, then you are more apt to create characteristics that support a feeling of inadequacy. As a result, you become self-critical and undermine your personality strengths. This is where knowing yourself intimately through personality is an advantage. Once you begin to understand why you do the things you do, then you can begin to accept and respect the uniqueness of your personality.

This book presents the concept that personality affects more than just your relationships. It offers the perspective that, in fact, personality impacts every aspect of your life, including the health and well-being of your physical body. Through this book, you will explore the connection between your personality and your health. You will discover how your personality can pre-dict weak sites, meaning specific areas in your body where you are more susceptible to creating illness.

Current research in the areas of behavioral medicine and psychoneuroimmunology reveals that there is a direct correlation between personality and illness. What these studies show is that it is the personality that creates the involuntary habits that determine how the mind/body chemically communicates. If a person's habits create a strong negative response, then their chances for creating illness increase significantly. For example, if you are always late, and being late causes you to feel bad about yourself or creates negative self-feedback, then every time you are late, you react by creating stress. That stress creates a negative chemical reaction in your body. If this habit continues over a prolonged period of time, then the negative chemical reaction "wears" down both your body

and your immune system and you become more susceptible to stress-related illnesses. As a matter of fact, there
are very predictable personality characteristics that can
predispose a person to hypertension, heart disease,
asthma, cancer, allergies, autoimmune disorders, and
many other related illnesses.

The book includes a personality assessment that will
allow you to determine if you are a RED, ORANGE, YEL-
LOW or GREEN personality type. It also features detailed
descriptions of each of the four personality colors, along
with information on each color's weak sites and potential health-related issues.

While it is important to understand other people's
personality type, it is even more important that you first
understand your own. Pay attention to your habits, why
you do the things you do, how you interact with others,
what your strengths are, and how you respond to life's
challenges. By doing so, you will begin to see what characteristics need to be changed. When you find yourself
coming up against the same old stumbling blocks and
something inside says, "Been there, done that," you are
being provided the opportunity to look at what needs
changing. If the changes you make are in alignment with
your personality boundaries, then you will not continue
to experience the same trouble spots.

For example, if you are a RED personality style and
your need to be in control is creating tremendous
amounts of stress, then you might consider releasing that
stress by doing something physical such as exercising or

participating in some form of athletic competition. If you are an ORANGE and find yourself always doing things for others and never having time for yourself, you might set aside time each week to pamper yourself, or learn yoga or meditation to help lessen your anxious reactions. If you are a YELLOW and find yourself frustrated by indecision because you can see both sides so clearly, create a mentally stimulating mind diversion such as playing a challenging computer game or reading a thought-provoking book. Or if you are a GREEN and get angry with yourself because your life is so disorganized and out of control, you might read books on how to manage time and how to get organized. Then, incorporate what you learn into your everyday lifestyle.

This book encourages you to discover your personality style, and it supports change change that will put you in a stronger position to create the life and health you desire and deserve. The rewards will be many, and the journey enlightening.

So, what color is your personality?

Chapter 1

Personality: It's in Your Genes

"Your personality, then, is the material expression.
And your individuality is the personality of the soul."
— Edgar Cayce

Have you noticed that you find yourself attracted to people who are similar to you? There is something subtle about them that magnetically attracts you to them. You feel comfortable with them, and you can relate to their thinking. They treat others in the same way *you* treat others, and you tend to make them a part of your social network and support system. These people are easy for you to communicate with, and they energize you when you are in their presence.

What about the people you meet or have to deal with who are opposite from you? You get messages that confirm that there is not good chemistry between you, that there is something about them that makes you want to pull back and protect yourself. They drain your energy. The more time you have to spend with them, the greater your awareness becomes of the magnitude of those differences. You struggle to find a common ground on which you can communicate. These people see the world through different eyes, and you realize that they even approach life from another perspective altogether. While it is true that opposites *do* attract, when it comes to building relationships with people who are opposite, the potential for conflict and misunderstanding is high. There will be difficulty finding a common understanding where one or the other does not feel compromised. In order to make these relationships work, each person must be willing to acknowledge and deal with their differences. Each must be willing to commit both time and energy to the relationship—not an easy task unless each becomes aware of why they act the way they do and why they differ.

What is it about people that makes one different from another? What gives each person their own unique individual behavioral characteristics? Why is it that we want to be around people who are like us and have difficulty dealing with people who are opposite? The answer to these questions is two-fold. The first answer has to do with how we energetically disclose ourselves to others. The second has to do with personality.

Each of us externally transmits our own "fingerprint" pattern of energy that communicates to others who we are. That pattern of energy is our personality. When we meet people who are similar in energy pattern and personality, we are attracted to them. When people who are not similar in energy or personality come into our lives, we may at first be attracted to them, yet we soon recognize their differences. If we can cope with or live with the differences, then we will work at building a relationship. However, if we choose not to deal with the differences, we will move on and seek others who are like ourselves. So, while opposites do attract, they do not necessarily stay together. Sometimes the differences are too great to overcome or do not justify the energy needed to deal with them.

It is within the mental layer of energy that our personality first reveals itself. That is because the core part of our personality determines our mental functioning. Every aspect of who we are physically and energetically is governed in some way by our personality. Personality has two aspects: inherited and learned. Inherited we cannot change. Learned we can change.

Personality Traits and Characteristics

Each one of us is born with inherent personality traits, meaning our biological genetic coding, which determine the way our brain develops and how our personality expresses itself. That is our core part. Our personality traits reveal themselves at a very early age and remain constant throughout our entire lives. They direct the way we act and how we think, and they establish our learned personality characteristics. Traits create our involuntary habits that determine the course our lives will take. They decide our preferred way of gathering information and how we draw conclusions from the information we take in.

Personality traits influence the choice of words we use to communicate with others, as well as how we learn. Our personality traits are responsible for our brain functioning and its normal neurobiological and biochemical reactions. They establish the electrochemical dialogue that takes place between the brain, the endocrine system, and the physical body. Personality traits reveal themselves through a predominant color found in the human energy system.

The learned parts of personality are called characteristics. Characteristics are the behavioral patterns that we develop as a result of what we have learned. They reflect our biographical history, and they are what makes us unique. They are the distinguishing qualities that differentiate us from others, and they establish our identity and how we express that identity to the outside world. Characteristics are responsible for the formation of habits, comfort zones, quirks, and idiosyncratic behavioral patterns. In the human energy system, our personality characteristics are reflected within the emotional layer of energy. They provide the biographical information that reveals itself through our emotional reactions.

When you combine personality traits and character-istics, you define personality type, meaning the consis-tent, predictable patterns that drive the way we live and why we act the way we do. Personality type represents the orderly arrangement through which we form our per-ceptions, attitudes, beliefs, and values. Using the premise of personality type as a categorical formula makes it eas-ier to understand and identify why people are different.

Think of your personality type as your automatic pilot. It creates the involuntary behavioral patterns nec-essary for you to function and survive. Its inherent traits create your own personal road map, which guides the outward direction you take in life. Its characteristics influence what you become. It affects your self-image, self-esteem, self-confidence, and self-worth. It motivates you, creates your irritations, and controls stress and how that stress affects you. Personality impacts the way you face life's challenges and the coping mechanisms you develop. It is the organizing principle that affects your sense of reality and spirituality. It greatly impacts your health and overall sense of well-being.

The History of Personality Type

For centuries, psychologists, psychiatrists, and physicians have studied personality. They have provided conclusive evidence that human beings do have distinct personality traits and characteristics that make them different from one another, and that personality affects both mental health and physical health. The first person to classify personality by type was Hippocrates, the father of Western medicine. He proposed that there were four distinct personality types. His theory was that a person's personality type determines their vulnerability to mental dysfunction and their susceptibility to illness. Ever since he declared his findings, there have been many others who have formed their own theories around personality and illness.

In the 19th century, psychoanalyst Sigmund Freud developed his own detailed theory of personality. His underlying assumption was that the body is the sole source of mental energy. He approached personality only from the mental perspective. Soon after Freud's theory was made public, psychiatrist Carl Jung proposed his own comprehensive theory to explain how personality type affects every aspect of a person's life. Unlike Freud,

Jung integrated the aspect of spirituality into his theory because of his own beliefs and background. He suggested that behavior was not random, but in fact, predictable, and therefore could be classified and observed. Like Hippocrates, Jung postulated that there were four personality types dominated by four distinct modes of psychological functioning: thinking, feeling, sensing, and intuition. While we do have the capacity to use all four of these functions, he theorized, we do not develop them equally.

Jung also believed that people are multisensory in their psychological functioning and do not rely on just the five senses (sight, hearing, touch, taste, smell) for the gathering of information. Jung was of the opinion that the differences in people were the result of inherited core psychological functions associated with how a person gathers information and makes decisions. Through his work, he became aware of basic attractions and aversions that people have toward other people, and he noticed that those same attractions

and aversions also related to tasks and life events. The more Jung worked with his theory, the better he understood what drives behavior, and the easier it was for him to see personality patterns that make people different.

According to most of the personality theories, we each have within our own personality type both strengths and weaknesses that are primarily determined by the genetic neurological hard-wiring found within our personality traits. The more we function within our inherent traits (strengths), the stronger and more confident we become, the stronger our sense of reality, the more control we have over our lives, and the better equipped we are to make the choices that create the life and health we want. We are in a stronger position to take advantage of and maximize the opportunities that life sets before us.

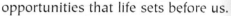

If we function outside our core traits and work from our underdeveloped psychological functions (weaknesses), then life loses its synchronicity. We become energetically drained, mentally confused, and experience physical discom-

fort. Our lives feel as if they are out of control, and we have a strong sense of being detached from life. We feel emotionally numb, and our thinking becomes fuzzy. We become mentally immobilized and chemically out of balance. These chemical imbalances create a fight-or-flight stress reaction in the physical body, and that stress response hinders our ability to think clearly to an even greater extent. As a result, we find ourselves caught up in a vicious cycle of psychological and emotional behavioral patterns that prevent us from getting where we want to go. In the end, we leave ourselves vulnerable to the creation of illness.

The Mind-Body Connection

Edgar Cayce stated, "The spirit is life. Mind is the builder. Physical is the result." Cayce, like many others, believed that what we think is what our body generally becomes. What we have learned is that the mind is the controller of all behavioral and physical functioning, and that the power of the mind can intentionally or unintentionally affect both the energy body and the physical body. In other words, we can make ourselves healthy

or
sick through our
thoughts and our emotional
reactions to those thoughts. Since
those early research studies, more comprehensive studies have taken place to further
the understanding of how the mind influences
our physical well-being. These studies are validat-
ing the premise that there is a direct correlation
between personality, thoughts, emotions, and illness.
What has been discovered is that our thoughts and
emotions are intertwined, and both play a significant role
in the development of disease. If our thoughts are charged
with positive energy, then we are emotionally optimistic
about life, and we experience an overall sense of well-
being. If our thoughts are negatively charged, then we rob
the physical body of the energy it needs to maintain balance. Negative thoughts provoke negative emotions:
fear, anger, frustration, worry, resentment, and
guilt—all of which have an undesirable and
potent effect on our ability to fight off disease
and infection. Negative thoughts wear
down both the energy system
and the immune system,
leaving a person

more susceptible to illness. Those same studies show that prolonged stress also wears down both the energy body and physical body and consequently impacts why people become ill and why they do not heal.

To better understand the mind-body connection, it helps to remember that the human brain is electrical in nature. It communicates its messages to specific sites in the body by sending electrochemical impulses via the central nervous system. These electrochemical impulses and the information they contain activate cellular memory and tell the cellular structure within that specific area of the body how to reorganize itself according to the information being received. If a person is thinking a negative thought, that consequently creates a negative emotional reaction. Then, the brain responds by changing the chemistry in the electrical impulses it sends to the body's systems. These changes in chemistry are what alert the physical body that there is a problem.

Let's say that people's thoughts continually dwell on being sick and tired of their lives. The electrochemical message sent from the brain to the body is that they are sick and tired. If the thought is emotional and is strongly supported, then the body intensifies its reaction by feeling sick and tired. The stronger the thought, the stronger the chemical reaction, and the greater the chances for severe illness to occur. Understanding how the mind electrochemically dialogues with the body makes it easier to see the direct correlation between state of mind and physical health.

It is important to note that not all thoughts—even those that have a slightly negative undertone—cause illness in the body. If our thoughts are positive and produce positive emotional reactions, then our physical body will continue to function as a healthy, vital unit. It is only the thoughts with strongly negative charges that affect the body and make it susceptible to disease.

To show what I mean, let's use cancer as an example. Psychoneuroimmunology, the study of how emotions affect the immune system, indicates that people who are consumed with negative thoughts or who have a negative outlook on life are more susceptible to the formation of cancer. The same holds true for people who are consumed with negative emotions such as fear, anger, or frustration. Negativity wears down the immune system and leaves the body more susceptible to the creation of disease. On the other hand, people who are optimistic and view life from a positive perspective have stronger immune systems and are able to resist infection and the formation of diseases such as cancer. What has been discovered is that when it comes to good health, positive thoughts play an important role. It also appears that a happy-go-lucky attitude can go a long way in fighting off disease and keeping us healthy.

The Personality and Physical Weak Sites

My own research confirms many of the same findings. It has continually demonstrated that there is a direct connection between personality, the human energy system, and wellness. It not only substantiates what research has revealed about how a person's mental state influences their susceptibility toward illness, it has also identified that each personality type has its own specific "weak site" within the physical body. Those weak sites are determined by psychological and emotional patterns created by a person's inherent personality traits. In fact, there are relatively specific personality traits that predispose a person to the creation of specific diseases, such as high blood pressure, heart disease, cancer, asthma, tuberculosis, autoimmune disorders and neurological diseases, as well as chronic related illnesses.

By understanding personality type and its associated psychological functioning, we can begin to understand the patterns of behavior that create illness. Through the identification of weak sites, we can determine where the origin of illness will manifest itself in the body. Since I am able to see the energy system and work with the body from the inside out, I have also found that, interestingly enough, a person's personality weak site tends to correspond to their biological weak site. It is within the weak sites that I can identify the origin of illnesses and have a better understanding of how other parts of the body will be affected. The primary difference between the way the energy system and the physical body communicate illness is that the physical body will put up symptoms anywhere in the body, and the energy system pinpoints precisely where the weak site and the root cause of the illness are located.

What I have found is that each personality type's weak site appears to be more sensitive to chemical imbalance than any other part of the body. Part of the reason for this is because of the control that our personality traits have on our psychological functioning and how that functioning affects the brain's biochemistry. In many ways, it is our personality that tells the brain how to electrochemically communicate with the body. Taking that premise one step further and connecting the weak sites with specific endocrine glands, organs, and bodily systems, it becomes easier to understand why people become ill in specific areas of the body. It is through our thoughts that we change the chemistry of our body in such a way that it can cause illness to manifest in our weak sites.

My research on personality also stems from the premise that there are four distinct personality types. Each of the four types is determined by their genetic personality coding and how that coding forms their neurological hardwiring. Each personality type's coding system is what determines their preference toward specific psychological functioning and how that functioning creates the patterns of behavior they exhibit. It is their preferred psychological functioning that delineates the differences in people and the way they gather information and draw conclusions. To help you better understand how personality type affects the body, let me share the session I had with Betty.

Betty—Age 25

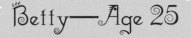

Betty came to see me to find out why she was not able to rid herself of a chronic lower back problem. She said she had experienced this problem her entire life. While she regularly went to a chiropractor for adjustments, she just ended up back where she started. The session revealed that her personality type is that of a caretaker and a worrier. Her energy system revealed that her personality weak site was her lower abdomen and lower back. Her caretaking patterns of behavior consistently drove her to want to care for the emotional needs of the people in her life. She was so driven by these patterns that she would take care of their needs before even thinking about taking care of her own. The emotional neediness of others burdened her, and she felt as if she were carrying everyone on her back.

Another personality pattern of behavior that Betty displayed was that of being a worrier. She worried about everything. In fact, worrying had become such a habit that there were times when she did not even know what she was worrying about. Betty worried about whether she would have enough energy to emotionally support those who needed it. She worried about whether she was doing a good job at work. She worried about whether she would have enough money to pay her bills even though she had gotten two pay raises in one year. She worried about being pulled in too many directions. She worried about not having enough money to live on when she retired. Her worries about retirement were interesting, since she was only 25 years old. I asked her about this, and she said the reason she was worrying was that her parents did not have enough retirement money, and she had to support them financially as well as herself.

All of the behavioral patterns associated with her personality type put her at risk for creating some kind of illness in her weak site. In fact, it was her worrying that was the root cause of her back problems—not surprising, since worry is a strong negative emotion and one that creates stress and chemical imbalance in the body. That chemical imbalance built up in her lower back and created so much muscle tension that her muscles were constantly pulling in opposite directions, thus putting pressure on the spine and causing it to continually be out of alignment. Her body finally reached a state physically and energetically where it could not carry any more and ended up creating chronic problems in the lumbar part of the spine. Interestingly enough, it was Betty's worrying about being pulled in different directions that her body responded to. It also became pulled in different directions and resulted in the lower back problem—another strong validation that the connection between personality and the human energy system affects how the mind and body communicate.

A Shift in Thinking

Partly due to current research findings, Western medicine is finally beginning to understand and embrace the idea that there is a connection

between mind and body. Physicians are starting to recognize that in order to truly heal someone, they must deal with both the disease and the mental state of the person, and must treat the cause as well as the symptoms. More and more physicians are encouraging patients to see diagnosticians such as medical intuitives and holistic practitioners, who can help them understand how their patterns of behavior influence their health. These practitioners can also teach them how to change their thoughts, and modify destructive behavioral patterns that have the potential to create illness. While the processes that the practitioners use are not new or particularly innovative, more and more they are being proven effective. Some of these techniques include meditation, breathing exercises, visualization, and affirmations. These processes greatly improve a person's ability to control and channel their thoughts in a positive way, thus improving their physical health. The benefit of embracing this healing perspective and incorporating these techniques into our daily

routines is that the root cause of the illness can be removed so that permanent healing can take place.

Your Relationship with You

I hope this chapter has helped to clarify which relationship may be the most important one you will ever build in your life. That is the relationship with *yourself*. As children, we are taught to focus our attention on building relationships with others and getting along with different people. We are encouraged to ignore others' quirks and idiosyncrasies and learn to live, love, and work with them. What we are not taught is how to love ourselves, how to look beyond our own quirks and imperfections, or how to change the habits we have formed that we do not like about ourselves or that tend to not serve us well.

I believe that through learning more about personality type, you can develop your own framework to better understand yourself. You will be able to recognize, comprehend, and utilize your personality strengths in such a way that you can maximize your innate capabilities and talents. You

will have a deeper understanding of how your mind and body communicate, and you will become aware of where your weak site is. You will begin to recognize which thoughts and patterns of behavior are self-destructive and create chemical imbalances that increase your potential for illness.

At a deeper, more spiritual level, the understanding of your personality type positions you to give power to your individuality as expressed through the personality of your soul. You experience a sense of wholeness that only comes through the unconditional integration of body, mind, and spirit. Your true essence and authenticity will reveal itself through the

lights of your aura for all to see and enjoy. You will experience the greatest, purest joy that there is in life—the joy that comes from accepting and loving yourself.

Reflection

We are, to the world, a physical presence and a personality presence. We learn to deal with issues around our physical presence from the day we are born. Our personality presence impacts our lives to a greater extent, and frequently we are oblivious to that impact.

Chapter 2

Color and Personality

"Color is inward and alive. Indeed the men of science tell us that it is an intense vibration, almost a quick pulsation of life itself."
— Vincent McNabb, author of *The Wayside*

The role that color plays in our lives is far more powerful than most of us may imagine. Color literally influences all aspects of who we are, both internally and externally. It affects us emotionally, psychologically, and physically, and its energy surrounds us and interpenetrates us. It resonates within us and emanates from us. It is as much a part of our daily existence as breathing, eating, and sleeping. The life force of energy that we get from color is an integral component in our ability to maintain balance and stay healthy. In the human energy system, color serves as a vital communication link that reflects what is happening within all four layers of energy: spiritual, emotional, mental, and physical. It is through color or lack of it that a skilled intuitive can identify and classify illness in both the energy body and the physical body. For our energy system, color is food for the soul. It feeds our body, mind, and spirit.

While color does act as a perceptual stimulus, we can also simply enjoy its energy through our physical senses. We can bask in the warmth of the yellow rays of the sun; see beauty when we look at the red of a rose; and feel moved by the sight of clear blue skies, flaming orange sunsets, golden fields of wheat, green forests, and all of Earth's glorious colors. For the psyche, the beauty of color can inspire, uplift, and delight the human spirit. Emotionally, it can change our moods. It can provoke certain emotional responses and suppress others. It can make us blue, green with envy, or see red when angry. Color can stimulate or sedate, excite or calm. It can increase the temperature of the body, or it can make chills run up and down our spine. The effects that color has on us are innumerable, powerful, and very real.

Physically, the impact color has on the body, the endocrine system, and the autonomic nervous system is profound. For instance, red stimulates circulation, raises blood pressure, and creates a stress reaction that activates the release of adrenaline. It can create intestinal gas and constipation. The color orange aids in the digestive and metabolic systems by affecting how the pancreas and thyroid glands dialogue with each other. Yellow stimulates mental activity, activates motor nerves, and strengthens the cerebrospinal nervous system. Green heals and relaxes the body and stimulates activity in the heart and respiratory system. Basically, color can affect illness, the way the body repairs itself, mental and physical growth, and a person's overall state of health.

For decades, there has been interest in the effect that color has on our health. There have been numerous research studies that explore the important role that color plays in the field of medicine in the prevention and treatment of illness. What these studies have revealed is that the perceptual response to specific colors is the same in every person. It makes no difference what their culture, personality type, or life circumstance is. The only time that this was not the case was with people who were color blind. It appears that our response to color is inherited and is a part of our neurological hard-wiring. When we look at a color, that color registers in the brain. The brain then sends an electrical message to the pituitary gland telling it how we are to react to the color it received. The pituitary gland, in turn, sends out a chemical message to the endocrine glands of the body, telling them which hormones to secrete, how much to secrete, and how that specific part of the body is to react.

An example of how color affects us was demonstrated in a research project conducted by the University of California, Berkeley, in 1979 within the California prison system. Guards who were considered to be in top physical condition were chosen to perform exercises using heavy dumbbells. They were instructed to do as many curling exercises as they could. After performing these exercises, a blue screen was put in front of them, blocking their view of anything else. Even though they felt tired, they were able to repeat the number of exercises. The blue color, while calming, acted in such a way that it allowed them to pace themselves better. Some even went on to exceed their previous number of repetitions. However, when a pink screen was placed in front of them, blocking their view of everything else, they all experienced a drastic reduction in the number of repetitions they could perform. Their muscles became fatigued, and they complained of being energetically drained. The impact was so severe that many were not even able to pick up the dumbbells. All their aggressiveness and competitiveness was gone. This research confirmed the premise that color does have a strong impact on us and can actually change the chemistry of the body. What this project pointed out is that pink slows down the circulation to the muscles and tranquilizes the body.

Linking Color to Personality

Looking at his research on the nature of personality, it's obvious that Carl Jung believed in the symbolic power of color. He would encourage his patients to use color spontaneously to help them express their personality. He believed that integrating color into their everyday lives would influence their behavior. It was, however, Dr. Max Luscher and his research that took color and applied it to the psychological functioning of personality type. Dr. Luscher believed that colors have an emotional value, and that a person's reaction to color reveals their basic personality traits. His research provided conclusive evidence that specific colors create the same psychological, emotional, and physiological reaction in each person. While acknowledging that the measurement of emotions was not completely possible, he was able to measure the physical reaction of the body to specific colors. Working with the same premise that there are four different personality types, he developed a color test that could be used as a means of identifying the differences in people. What he learned about personality from the test results is that core personality preferences are organized into four color groups. The color name he gave to each group indicated the dominant organizing behavior around psychological functioning based on personality traits.

My own research delves even deeper into the relationship of color and personality and differs in some ways. The colors that I selected to represent the four personality types are representative of the totality of who we are. When I began looking at the predictable behavioral patterns found in personality type and connected those patterns of behavior to the psychological and emotional behavioral patterns associated with the four lower aspects of the human energy system, I discovered that they were inseparable. Then, taking the colors of the human energy system—red, orange, yellow, and green— and looking at the psychological and physiological effects they have on the body, I again found that there was a consistent correlation. Working from that premise, I developed an interest in how all of these elements revealed themselves in the human energy system. What I discovered is that not only are they all connected, but they are interdependent upon each other. All influence our health, determine why we become ill, and identify the weak sites within the body.

Colors and Characteristics

Using Carl Jung's findings that psychological functioning falls into four categories: sensing, intuition, thinking, and feeling, I applied the four colors—red, orange, yellow, and green—of the human energy system to indicate the dominant organizing behavior or information-gathering process of each personality type. Here is what I discovered:

1. **Red** personality types are *sensing, thinking* in their functioning. Their orientation to the world is through external stimuli, and their core mental functioning is left brain. They are literal and see things as black or white. They are the most physical of all personalities and need to experience, to express, to do, and to achieve goals. They are hardworking, ambitious people who are driven to conquer. With a traditional and conservative approach to life, they live more in the past than the present, and are concerned with personal safety and security. They are firm-minded, stubborn, and assertive, needing to control both their environment and the people in it. Inner conflict exists between the desire for power and status and the need to be left alone. Red energy stimulates all systems of the body. It represents aggression, passion, strength, and action. The color red excites and represents the blood of life.

2. **Orange** personality types are *sensing, feeling* in their functioning. Their orientation to the world is through people; thus, they thrive on being able to fulfill the emotional needs of others. Their core mental functioning is left-right brain, so they make decisions based on how they feel about things. Orange energy seeks harmony and cooperation between people, and focuses on family and on the building of relationships that are mutually beneficial. They are emotional people and will use these feelings as a means of getting others to do what they want. They live more in the present than the past. *Oranges* become threatened when their security is jeopardized—they are jealous and protective of their things and the people they care about. They are worriers and have a fear of not having enough. They seek social acceptance. Orange energy is friendly, welcoming, and approachable. It is a social, warm color. The color orange relates to desire and ambition.

3. **Yellow** personality types are *intuitive, thinking* in their functioning. Their core mental functioning is right-left brain. However, the yellow personality type is the only one of the four that is mentally hard-wired to utilize all four of the psychological functions equally. They are both conceptual and analytical thinkers who pride themselves on their ability to solve problems—the more complex the better. They live in both the present and the future, experiencing time as a continuous flow of processes. They thrive on novelty and mental excitement, yet remain emotionally detached from people and situations. Their heightened sense of self and their need for independence and autonomy make them difficult to get to know. Yellow in the energy system reflects intellect and is a synthesis of both linear thinking and creativity. Its energy stimulates the mind. Yellow energy triggers creativity so one is stimulated to take on new challenges and explore new directions. Emotionally, from a positive perspective, yellow represents optimism and joy. Negatively, it represents lack of courage and fear of criticism.

4. **Green** personality types are *intuitive, feeling* in
    their functioning. Their orientation to the world
    is toward people and the need for relation-
    ships. Their core functioning is right-brained.
    They are expansive in their thinking—idea
    people who thrive on change and are constant-
    ly seeking new experiences. They are idealis-
    tic—they march to their own drummer, yet
    have a real need to fit in and find their com-
    munity. They are continually hopeful and opti-
    mistic that they will find their place in society,
    since they need conflict-free environments and
    relationships, and are driven by their need to
    be liked. *Greens* seek energetic social contact
    and approval. They live in the past and future
    rather than in the present; consequently, they
    are seen as being disconnected from reality.
    They are continually impatient with the pres-
    ent because it is too slow to catch up with
    their futuristic thinking. They have a deep
    longing for spiritual fulfillment. In the human
    energy system, green is the heart color; there-
    fore, green personalities are heart people. The
    color of wholeness, green energy promotes the

balance of intuition with emotions. It represents the path to self-love and self-esteem. Physically, it affects metabolism and acts as self-regulating energy for the heart. Green acts as a stimulant to the respiratory system, encouraging us to breathe as a means of maintaining balance, both physically and mentally. Energetically, green acts as an antihistamine and decongestant to unclog and remove blockages from within the energy body.

My work, as well as that of others, shows us that personality and its psychological functions drive the way we think, how we act, and why we develop the patterns of behavior we do. The four-color formula that I present to you in this book is a synthesis of all the different aspects of who you are: energetically, emotionally, mentally, and physically. It is meant to provide a comprehensive model of looking at yourself and guiding you toward a better understanding of what you can do to have both a healthy personality and a healthy body. By understanding what controls and directs you, you will be in a better position to make the choices and changes in your life that move you toward what you desire instead of repeating behavioral patterns that prevent you from getting what you want. Your ability to heal yourself rests largely upon knowing what you need to do to free yourself from the patterns of behavior that can potentially lead to illness.

While I understand that there are risks and limitations that come with categorizing people, the four-color formula is an effective way of creating an awareness of the differences in people. It is not my intention to take away any person's individuality or uniqueness. It is, however, my intention to show you that while each of us is unique, we still share common predictable patterns of behavior. I believe that the four-color formula is a tool that can help us better understand the complexity of human behavior and why we become ill.

The value of using color as a means of looking at personality is that it is nonthreatening. We all respond to color in much the same way, so it provides a basis for a common understanding. Besides, color is the universal language that bridges the physical and spiritual realms.

Reflection

*There is a connection
between the way our
thinking processes work,
and our personalities. That
connection can be identified
by a color, which ties
directly to the colors of the
human energy system. Color
then becomes an identifier
of personality type, mental
processing, behavioral
tendencies, and wellness.*

Chapter 3

What Color Is Your Personality?

"To know thyself is the beginning of wisdom."
— Socrates

How can you tell your personality color or the personality colors of others if you are not able to see the energy field of the body? That question led me to develop the Personality Color Indicator (PCI) system. The PCI talks to the brain in such a way that it can be used as a means of identifying core personality traits that determine our psychological functioning, how we gather information, and how we draw conclusions or make decisions.

The PCI's primary purpose is to delineate the differences in behavioral patterns that are consistent from one personality type to another. The value of the PCI system is that it allows you to see yourself from a different perspective—the perspective of color. It is designed to provide a better understanding of why you think and act the way you do. The information that surfaces through the PCI can become the framework for you to better understand how to tap into and utilize your natural talents, strengths, and capabilities. Its information helps you explore the connection between your actual and perceived self so you can get a better sense of the direction you might take in your life. It brings forth valuable insight into the relationship you have with yourself and with others. It also provides an understanding of the differences in people and how those differences affect you.

What the Personality Color Indicator is not, is an instrument to determine the state of a person's mental health, the presence of personality disorders, a measurement of intelligence, or an evaluation of emotional stability. Like a mirror, it is simply a tool that provides a reflective approach to seeing yourself in a different way.

When looking at all the different aspects of personality, there are two other factors that should be at least discussed and taken into consideration. Those are the factors of introversion and extroversion, which influence how people interact and how they express themselves. They also impact how we first see people and how we energetically relate to them. While the PCI system does not identify these two factors in the assessment, I have included them in the type descriptions to show that two people can have the same personality color, and yet their introversion or extroversion factors can make them appear quite different. The reason for not including them in the assessment is that they do not directly impact the connection between personality, the energy system, and the human energy system; also, they tend to change throughout the cycles we experience in life. The PCI system is only interested in core personality functioning and how that functioning affects the communication link between mind and body, and specifically the endocrine and nervous systems of the body.

While it is true that all of us are a little bit of each personality color, what I have discovered is that people

and habitual patterns, circle the letter to its left. If you do not agree, go on to the next statement.

A 1. I consider myself to be down-to-earth.

A 2. I prefer to stick to a set daily routine rather than put myself in unfamiliar situations.

B 3. I enjoy using my creativity to come up with innovative ways of doing things rather than doing them the way that everyone else does.

A 4. I stay focused and concentrate on what needs to be completed now rather than thinking about future tasks.

B 5. I become bored with tasks that are repetitious and find myself looking for different and better methods of doing them.

B 6. I enjoy the challenge of finding solutions to problems that are complex and that need to be explored from a variety of perspectives.

A 7. I consider myself to be practical, not theoretical.

B 8. I have a lot of thoughts in my head simultaneously, and I am often accused of not listening or of being preoccupied.

A 9. I would rather work with facts and figures than theories and ideas.

B   10. I pride myself on using my intellect and being a creative problem solver.

A   11. I would rather deal with the known than explore possibilities.

B   12. I prefer being original rather than traditional.

B   13. I am interested in how machines and products work so I can come up with ways to improve them.

B   14. I prefer learning new skills more than using old ones.

A   15. I am detail oriented.

A   16. I find myself attracted to people who are similar to me: realistic, practical, and involved with current issues.

A   17. I become impatient and frustrated with problems or tasks that are too complicated.

B   18. I prefer to read books that provoke thought and allow the mind to wander and explore a variety of scenarios.

A   19. I would rather follow standard operating procedures than create new ways of doing things.

A   20. I want work tasks and time expectations clearly defined before I begin a project.

B   21. I am usually on a different wavelength from most people.

B 22. I tend to answer questions with a question in order to gather more information.

A 23. I interpret things literally rather than conceptually.

A 24. I am more interested in the production and distribution of products than in their design and application.

B 25. I thrive on variety and dislike repetition.

B 26. I am a risk-taker and shun the conservative approach to life.

A 27. I look for tried and proven ways to solve problems and rely on past experiences, rather than wasting my time seeking new and unproven solutions.

B 28. I enjoy listening to new ideas and exploring their potential rather than dealing with the mundane.

B 29. I would rather create with my mind than produce with my hands.

A 30. When confronted with a problem, I react quickly rather than dwelling on it before doing anything.

D 31. I will suppress my own feelings rather than hurt the feelings of others.

D   32. I go overboard for people and overextend myself to meet their needs, even at my own expense.

C   33. I do not show my feelings easily and have been told that I am hard to get to know.

C   34. I would rather deal with task problems than people problems.

C   35. I resolve conflicts based on what is fair rather than being concerned with feelings.

D   36. I find that people tend to take advantage of my good nature and kindheartedness.

C   37. I react with logic rather than emotion.

C   38. I make decisions based on logic rather than emotions.

C   39. I rarely seek advice from others before I make a decision.

D   40. I warm up to people easily and would not want to be thought of as cold and indifferent.

D   41. I prefer a work environment where there is no conflict and where people are appreciated and praised for what they contribute.

C   42. I am critical by nature and express my opinions freely.

D   43. I show my feelings easily.

D   44. I am accepting of others, not judgmental.

D 45. I expect those close to me to be sensitive to my feelings and emotional ups and downs, and I feel hurt when they are not.

D 46. I resolve conflicts by asking people for their advice so that I can gain reassurance and confidence in my decisions.

C 47. I stay calm, cool, and collected in situations where others are reacting emotionally.

D 48. I am good at resolving people problems.

C 49. I am a perfectionist and like things done the right way—my way.

C 50. I am more task oriented than people oriented.

D 51. I am more concerned with making good decisions than right decisions.

C 52. I would rather work with someone who is reasonable and responsible than with someone who is thoughtful and kind.

D 53. I am a peacemaker, not an aggressor.

D 54. I tend to be overly sympathetic to the needs of people.

C 55. I am more interested in solving problems than dwelling on them.

C 56. I deal with people issues in a straightforward manner and call them like they are.

D 57. It is important to promote good feelings and harmony within my relationships.

C 58. I think that it is more important to be respected than to be liked.

D   59. I am good at creating a team atmosphere and getting others to rally around a common goal or cause.

C   60. I show how much I care for someone by being responsible and conscientious rather than being emotional and sentimental.

Total the letters circled:

A_____   B_____   C_____   D_____

Add **A** and **C** together.
Add **B** and **C** together.
Add **A** and **D** together.
Add **B** and **D** together.

RED   YELLOW

A + C _____   B + C _____

ORANGE   GREEN

A + D _____   B + D _____

Your highest numerical score denotes your pre-disposition for that particular color type. If your score is particularly high in your color type, it indicates that you are strongly influenced by the characteristics and patterns of behavior associated with that type. If your numbers are close, they indicate flexibility within your type. It is not unusual if your color type is green to have numbers very close in more than one other color, because *greens* are the chameleons of the personality world. It is also not unusual for green and orange numbers to be close. The reason for this is that both make decisions based on emotions. The same holds true for reds and yellows, since both make decisions based on logic. Also, please note that your numerical scores may change depending on what is happening in your life. However, your strongest color type will remain consistent no matter what challenges life places on your path.

Note: Each of us regularly uses all of the mental processes identified in the Personality Color Indicator. However, we do not use all of them equally well. The objective of the PCI system is to identify your preferred core personality traits as they relate to your information-gathering and decision-making processes.

Please remember that no color is better or worse than any other. Use the information that surfaces through the PCI as a tool to help you better understand who you are and how you relate to others. Using this information as a foundation to build from, you can strengthen your innate qualities and readjust the behavioral patterns that both prevent you from getting what you want, and affect your health in a negative way. My greatest desire is that you will use this information as a way of learning how to appreciate and accept the differences in people. Just keep in mind that your weakness may be someone else's strength. And that, collectively, those differences can create mutually beneficial relationships.

Reflection

Our core personality traits define who we are, how we gather information, and how we make decisions. In this complex world of family, social, casual, and work-related interactions with people, we are constantly reminded that we are not all the same.

The first step in recognizing that there are differences is to understand why those differences exist. The second step is to accept that differences are just that—differences— nothing more, nothing less.

Chapter 4

The Red Personality

"Red stirs the senses and passions."
— Dr. Morton Walker, author of *The Power of Color*

The words that best describe *reds* are *practical, realistic, down-to-earth, sensible, pragmatic,* and *dependable.* Traditionalist in their beliefs and values, *reds* are the backbone of society. They believe that people should earn their way in life through hard work and service to others. Rigidly conscientious, they

approach everything from a no-nonsense point of view. *Reds* see the world for exactly what it appears to be—what you see is what you get. Loyal to their families, their causes, and their superiors, they operate best within traditional power structures where everyone knows their place. They are sensitive to lines of authority and are rigid about staying within those lines. Even if *reds* do not agree with rules or procedures, they will not challenge them. They accept them for what they are and understand that without structure and guidelines, there would be *chaos*.

Reds are masters at managing the everyday realities of life. They do what needs to be done, moving ahead even when resources are limited. Their motto is "Get it done, don't make excuses, and learn to work with what you have." Once *reds* set their minds to doing something, they refuse to be distracted by people and problems that might impede their progress. They believe that there are specific ways in

which things should be done. And, to ensure that things are done their way, they will create rules and expect others to follow them. *Reds*, by nature, are not risk takers, and if they must take risks, it will be only after careful consideration. They prefer to act on what they know, and stay with the tried and true rather than doing something for the first time or doing something that has never been done before. Their world is tangible. If you cannot see it, hear it, touch it, taste it, or smell it, then it is not real. Binary in their approach to life, they see a right way and a wrong way and nothing in between. They need tasks and projects well defined; otherwise, they become stressed and feel out of control. They are most comfortable in relationships and environments where they are in control and know what is going on at all times.

Reds are rapid-fire thinkers and become impatient with too much planning. They set concrete objectives and work hard to reach those objectives as quickly and directly as possible. They do not see value in analyzing a situation to death, preferring to act and get things done. *Reds* are literal in their interpretation of things—everything is black or white. Gray areas and ambiguity are not comfortable for them; intangibles have very little value in a *red's* world. For them, spending time exploring possibilities and creating ideas that are nonproductive or that may not go anywhere is a total waste of time. They are not abstract thinkers, and, in fact, have very little patience with people who are. This is not to say that they are not idea people—they are, but unless they have some assurance that the idea will work prior to moving forward, they will view it as a waste of time, and wasting time does not sit well with them. *Reds* see their role in the creative process as that which gives it substance and turns ideas into reality.

Reds have a need to control—both their environment and the people in it. They believe that if they are in control, then they can somehow buffer themselves from life's surprises, which they so dislike. They do not give compliments easily, believing instead that people must earn them. *Reds* tend to focus on what is wrong with people rather than focusing on their positive qualities. They are known for berating others for their negative behavior and yet not ever seeing their own behavior as negative. Autocratic and dictatorial in their interaction with others, they are highly effective at using intimidation and aggression in order to get what they want. Their need to dominate is so strong that they are often accused of being insensitive to the feelings and needs of others; however, that is not the case. *Reds* see their domination of others as a means of teaching, of helping them to be better. They see others who think differently as difficult to get along with or simply argumentative. They are strong, forceful personalities who are driven by the need for power and status.

Reds are fiercely competitive. In their rush to win, they may simply push others aside or run over them. They will not back down from a confrontational situation, seeing compromise as defeat. They thrive in competitive environments and use competition as a means of motivation. *Reds* view themselves as survivalists. For them, winning is everything—no matter how high the price or how demanding the conditions, they will not be squeamish in their quest for winning or being on top. If winning means stepping on others to get what they want, then so be it. They do not identify with the underdogs nor do they have a need to feel sorry for them. From the *red* perspective, there can only be one winner, and that winner will be them. In their reality, the more challenging or ferocious the competition, the more stimulating it is. They prefer taking the offensive position rather than the defensive or passive position.

Hard work is the hallmark of *reds*—they make things happen. Driven by a need for completion, they will not rest until the job is done; only then can they justify time off to play. They work hard and play hard, rolling up their sleeves and jumping right in. *Reds* pride themselves on their ability to manage people, deal with facts, and solve problems. They are detail oriented, and for them, no detail is too small to overlook. They need structure in both their lives and work, and they are happiest working in environments where systems and procedures are well established. They need all tasks and expectations to be well defined and do not like wasting time. *Reds* are the kind of employees that every employer dreams of—loyal, steadfast, and dependable. They do not mind taking on routine or redudant tasks. They become resentful and feel their time is being wasted in meetings where there is no agenda, or that are open-ended. Being involved in conversations that are not going anywhere is a major thorn in their side. *Reds* do not work well in environments where they have to guess at what needs to be done; rather, they need to know precisely what their tasks and responsibilities are, and how their performance is going to be measured. They need others to tell them what, when, and why. They do not like to fill in the blanks because someone else forgot to tell them everything. Needing to see immediate results from their efforts, their motto in life is, "Just do it."

Since *reds* are hard workers, they expect the same of others. They have little tolerance for people who make excuses or who are nonproductive, expecting people to keep their personal problems to themselves, and to definitely leave them at home. The work environment is no place for emotional issues. They measure on the bottom line, expect results, and do not place value merely on effort. They believe that everything depends on them, and that it is their responsibility to drive others to get things done. *Reds* will never be accused of being free-loaders, because they believe in earning their way. They have a strong work ethic and believe in giving a good day's work for a good day's pay.

Reds see what they do for a living as the means of identifying who they are because they live to work and work to live. Their work offers them the greatest opportunity to utilize and capitalize on their strengths. Job titles are important to *reds* because their titles let others know how successful they are. *Reds* who do not have (or believe they do not have) important titles or important jobs tend to suffer from low self-esteem. Their self-confidence level seems to be directly tied to their work and their position. For a *red* to be out of work is extremely uncomfortable and destructive to their overall confidence level, and being vulnerable creates anxiety and paranoia. Their need to provide for their families is so strong that when they are unable to fulfill these responsibilities, they become frustrated, angry, and prone to deep states of depression.

Reds want to belong and to serve. They need that consistency in their lives and relationships and do not like change unless they initiate it. They are driven by their sense of responsibility to provide the basic human necessities for their families, such as food, shelter, and clothing. They are firm believers in the need for rules that govern the interaction of people, whether they relate to family, work, city, school, or church. They are staunch disciplinarians, and their path in life is that of duty and dedication. They are drawn to jobs that are predictable

and
offer long-term security.

Reds are physical people. They are aggressive, active, rough-and-tumble individuals. They are physically assertive and enjoy participating in activities that involve physical contact. They tend to make good leaders because they know what it takes to get the job done. They also understand what it takes to make a good team and are not shy about pushing people to get the best performance out of them. They pursue life with gusto, vitality, and courage. They want to be involved in the game of life and are never comfortable sitting on the sidelines. The more intense and focused the activities, the happier they are. *Reds* will be the first to roll up their sleeves and dive into a project if the rewards are great enough.

At their best, *reds* are production machines. They are consistent in their behavior and are seen by others as the driving forces of progress. Once *reds* understand what needs to be done, get out of their way. They will bulldoze anything in their paths and are tireless in the pursuit of getting the job done. *Reds* will not sit around twiddling their thumbs waiting for others to make decisions. If things are going too slow for *reds*, they will provide whatever motivation is necessary to make things happen. Their greatest ability is to solve problems via the collection and assimilation of facts. Their mental processing is sequential and orderly. They believe in taking one step at a time, never making educated guesses. Methodical and painstaking in their attention to detail, *reds* look at all of the facts and base their decisions on those facts and historical precedent. If the facts substantiate their decision, then that decision becomes cast in concrete.

At their worst, *reds* are indecisive, overly cautious, abrupt, and argumentative. They become so focused on what is directly in front of them that they lose sight of any long-range view. They cannot see the forest for the trees. They are known to resolve problems too quickly just to get them out of their hair. If pressed to make a decision without what they consider adequate information, they become frustrated and contentious. They feel like they are out of control and consequently become rigid and resistant to any input from others. They just want to be left alone. Life becomes depressing, and reality becomes their worst nightmare. They become moody and pessimistic. Their need to control drives them to want to dominate others even more. That domination pushes others even farther away, leaving *reds* feeling isolated and unloved. At their very worst, *reds* play "poor me." They want others to feel sorry for them because they work so hard and carry so much of the burden of life. *Reds* can get so caught up in feeling sorry for themselves that they lose touch with reality. They become inefficient and nonproductive. When in this state of mind, *reds* see life as just one unpleasant thing after another. They become dissatisfied with everything and everyone. If really feeling out of control, *reds* become paranoid and think that everyone is out to get them or take what they have.

Extroverted Reds

Extroverted *reds* believe in making the most of the moment. They are doers who like to keep themselves involved in life. They like to keep things lively and churning as much as possible. This behavior keeps others off balance so *reds* feel like they are in control. Even though *reds* do not like change, they are known for changing direction midstream just to keep people on their toes. They do not rest on their laurels, and they make things happen however they need to. If extroverted *reds* decide that something needs to get done, either join in the effort and match their pace, or get out of their way. They are impatient and have difficulty relaxing if there are things that need to be done. Extroverted *reds* do not cope well with things that do not go their way. They need to control the activities and agenda. You either go along or you don't go at all.

Reds are outgoing, gregarious, straightforward, extremely direct, and vocal when it comes to expressing what they like or do not like. They do not pull any punches when it comes to telling others what they want and expect. They are masters at getting to the heart of matters. When they ask questions, they expect simple, direct answers. They have no tolerance for lengthy, complex explanations. If they ask you the time, give them only the time. They do not want to know how the watch was built.

Introverted Reds

Introverted *reds* are quiet, introspective, serious, matter-of-fact, reserved people who are reliable and steadfast. They are patient and painstakingly systematic in their approach to solving problems. Unlike their extroverted counterparts, they will not exert themselves any more than they have to. They do not enter into things impulsively. They do not see bulldozing ahead or butting heads with people as a good use of their time or energy. They are methodical in their approach to both life and tasks. To them, life is what you see and nothing more. No other types are more thorough, hardworking, or patient than introverted *reds*. Their perseverance and quiet presence tends to act as a stabilizer for others. They will not do anything that does not make sense. They enjoy quiet activities and solitude and prefer working by themselves rather than working with people. For introverted *reds*, people and their problems are distractions. They need a life that will give them the stability they need without emotional demands.

Reflection

The red's world is one of hard work,
realism, compliance, and stability.

Imagine an automobile, and the part
of it that each personality type
would identify with. The red would be
the motor and the driveline—
the parts of the auto that power it to
make it go. Reds move the world.

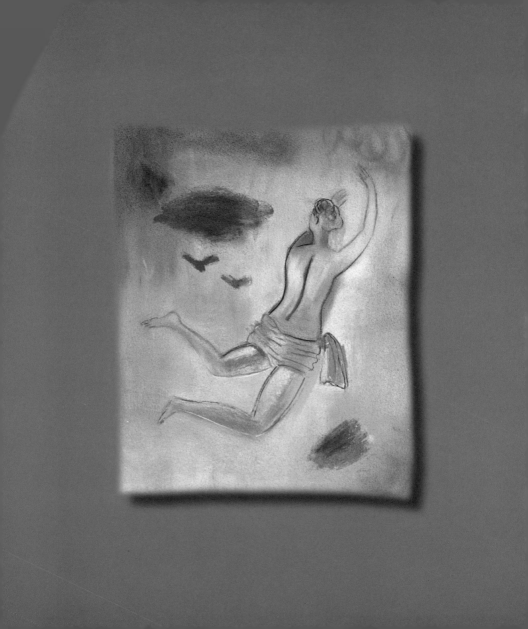

Chapter 5

The Orange Personality

"Orange is the social color of service to mankind."
— Alex Jones, author of *Seven Mansions of Color*

O*range* personalities are, by nature, caretakers. Caring for and about other people is what makes their lives worth living. Both men and women are especially attuned to the basic needs of the people in their lives, and will always put the needs of others before their own. You will not find another type who is more loving, more solicitous, more sensitive, or more concerned about basic human emotional needs than an *orange*. They are devoted and committed to those they care about, and of all types they are the most family-oriented—both to their blood families and to their work families. *Oranges* will instinctively assume the role of caretakers, and they take this responsibility very seriously. They work hard to maintain a balanced, comfortable, and emotionally nurturing environment. They feel it is their responsibility to do everything for other people so those people will be happy.

A good way to describe *orange*s is that they are mother hens, always wanting to protect their chicks. As the mother hen, they tuck their chicks under their wings until the chicks are strong and old enough to venture out on their own. *Oranges* fret and worry about the well-being of those they care about. They tend to make excuses for others and defend them. They see their role as that of the peacemaker.

At their best, *oranges* are devoted, considerate, and ever-so-helpful team players. For *oranges,* it makes no difference whether the team is family, work, church, a charitable organization, or the military. They have a strong sense of community and need to be involved in activities that will directly benefit themselves and those they care about. Crusaders who champion the rights of those less fortunate, they are socially responsible and expect others to be the same. *Oranges* bring a sense of tradition and provide good solid values, knowing that both of these are necessary to build a foundation for a strong, healthy society. Their lives focus on doing what is right and what is conventional. To *oranges*, the soundness of any good idea is not judged by the individual who created it, but by the outside community where it will positively affect the lives of others. It is not uncommon to find *oranges* in leadership capacities in either community projects or organizations if they believe their involvement will have an impact.

However, they are not always leaders on the job. They are dutiful and willing to relinquish authority if need be, always willing to help others. Since they are team players, their needs are the same as those of the group leader, and their happiness comes from the fulfillment of the directives and goals of others. What *oranges* will do in most workplaces is position themselves so they become the hub of information, and others will rely on them. When *oranges* do take the leadership position, they make things happen by gaining the cooperation and support

o f
others. They are natural
administrators and make task manage-
ment look easy. They are skilled at communicating the tasks that are necessary to get the job
done, and at communicating in such a way that people
freely cooperate and join in. *Oranges* expect and require others to be considerate of feelings and become dismayed when
they are not. If others let them down, *oranges* feel taken advantage
of and betrayed and react strongly. Then these usually polite, courteous people become very aggressive and outspoken.

Oranges love to bring people together. Social types, they seem to
make friends wherever they go. They enjoy entertaining—to an *orange* it
is an event, and they are willing to do things that will make other people feel at home, such as fixing favorite dishes for their guests. They
have a personal flair that is unique to their own type when entertaining. They entertain with one thought in mind, to make it fun for
everyone involved. If you get invited to an *orange's* party, you can
be sure that you will feel pampered. They love theme parties.
For example, if an *orange* throws a Hawaiian party, not
only will the food conform to the theme, but so will
the decorations and the attire. Their attention
to detail in party planning goes beyond
what most would think of.

Oranges are masters at creating an atmosphere where people can escape the realities of day-to-day life. As hosts, they are considerate of dietary needs, seeing that their guests are comfortable and that everyone is involved in the conversations and activities—always anticipating their guests' needs. They believe that the way to people's hearts is through caring and making life as enjoyable as possible. *Oranges*, while being somewhat serious by nature, know that laughter and the ability to laugh is the best medicine. They are good at making others laugh but often forget to laugh themselves.

Oranges are extremely sensitive to the feelings of others. They are good listeners, so others will seek them out to share their feelings and emotional hurts. *Oranges* have a knack for sorting out complex emotional problems and emotionally volatile situations. They are natural counselors. If you ever want to take a pulse of the emotional level in an environment, especially at work, talk to an *orange*. They make it their business to know where people are emotionally. You can always count on an *orange* to get a clear picture of people's attitudes, their likes and dislikes, who is having an emotional trauma, and who is not. *Oranges* are committed to creating a productive, harmonious environment, be it at work or at home.

    Oranges are naturally cautious and approach any kind of change with trepidation until they fully understand the implications and the impact the change will have on their lives, security, and family. *Oranges*, if given a choice, will never jeopardize themselves or those they love by taking unnecessary risks through reckless actions or careless thinking. *Oranges* are worriers. Consequently, they work very hard at trying to always be prepared. They will worry about anything and everything. They tend to live with a constant low-level anxiety about life and a vague apprehension that leaves them wary and overly cautious. Their first tendency will always be to stay within familiar comfort zones rather than taking risks or trying something new. They will procrastinate or postpone having to deal with change until they have time to see how it feels. If it feels right and they think it is in their best interests, they will not only embrace the changes, but they will make the changes work for the good of everyone.

    Oranges like their homes and their work environment to be tidy and orderly. Interestingly enough, an *orange* will accept disarray in others' lives but not in their own. *Oranges* can only handle disarray for a short period of time and then they become compelled to "get their house in order." Being out of order makes them moody and difficult to be around. They become depressed, show signs of frustration, and become emotionally agitated. This behavior is contradictory to their nature and is negative and destructive for them. When *oranges* are functioning effectively, they are competent and thorough. They are hardworking, patient, and extremely productive. They can move mountains if necessary to get things done. When functioning ineffectively, they are self-absorbed, stubborn, and brooding. They allow things to fall between the cracks. They start feeling sorry for themselves and wallow in self-pity. They will lash out and blame others for what is happening. To them, it is rarely their fault.

Oranges are courteous people unless crossed. It takes a lot to push an *orange* to the point where they will lash out at others, but when they do, there is no doubt in anyone's mind that the *orange* has reached their limit. When crossed, *oranges* become rigid and stubborn and express their emotional hostility vehemently. They lash out and use words that create instant anxiety and shock in others. When *oranges* unleash their rage, it will usually catch others so off guard that they will feel like a deer caught in headlights, about to get hit. If feeling pressed, *oranges* will become extremely temperamental, and emotionally fly off the handle at every little thing. Their emotional outbursts cause others to seriously question if they want be around them. At their worst, *oranges* become cynical, negative, and back-stabbing, and if they are feeling insecure, their behavior becomes erratic. *Oranges*, when stressed, are demanding. They hold grudges and do not easily forgive and forget. The best way to deal with *oranges* when they are in this mind-set is to allow them to get their feelings off their chests and then leave them alone for a while. This allows them time to reconcile their feelings with both their guts and their minds.

Oranges have a strong need for personal praise—even though when praised, they will usually respond by saying, "It was nothing."

Constant and tangible signs of reassurance is what gives *oranges* a sense of self-worth and self-confidence. They need to know they are appreciated and are an integral part of the team. With *oranges*, a simple, "job well done," will keep them motivated and productive. *Oranges* are always inquiring either directly or indirectly about others' feelings, office politics, or what is currently going on in people's lives. Keeping a finger on daily activities helps them feel secure and alleviates most of the fears they have of being left out or missing something that will have a direct impact on their security.

Oranges are careful to promote good feelings between themselves and the people who are important in their lives. They are polite, agreeable, and tactful. They are interested in creating environments that will encourage people to be productive. They will usually create committees to deal with issues. They are always looking for ways to involve people as the means of making things happen. They will try to solve problems by working to understand the perspectives of the people involved. They will hold private meetings with those involved in order to obtain the vital data necessary to make decisions. *Oranges* use this process so they can get a clear picture of how decisions will affect the group collectively. They are sympathetic toward the personal problems of others.

Oranges dislike conflict and will work hard to avoid it. However, unlike their emotional counterparts, *greens*, they will not shy away from it, even if it requires compromising their traditional values or time with their families. *Oranges* more than any other type struggle with the balance between work and home. On the one hand, they are loyal employees and take their jobs seriously, and on the other hand, they are driven by the needs of their family. *Oranges* are willing to work hard and put in long hours if that is what is required to get the job done. But do not expect them to make a habit of it.

Oranges also tend to be physical people, but they are not driven competitively, as are *reds*. Where *reds* will bulldoze their way forward no matter what, *oranges* understand their limits and the boundaries of those limitations. Instead of pushing forward head-on into obstacles, they will listen to what their gut tells them. They will step back and evaluate what price they will have to pay to accomplish the desired results. If the results do not justify the risk to them or to those they care about, they will back away. *Reds'* interpretation of this type of behavior is that *oranges* are not committed. The truth is that *oranges* are just more sensitive.

Oranges manage their resources well and plan for the future. For them, having money means that they can make the choices they want in life. They believe that financial stability is their only security. They enjoy the accumulation of material possessions. They plan for retirement so they will not have to worry about their security. They want to be able to help their children and to send them to good schools. *Oranges* are frugal and save money throughout their lives. It is important to them to make sure their financial resources will be sufficient when they retire so they can continue to live a comfortable lifestyle. They want to have flexibility to do as they please and go where they want. When you ask *oranges* what they plan to do when they retire, it will usually involve some kind of community activity that will benefit others, such as volunteering.

An *orange's* self-esteem is directly tied to and influenced by the quality of their relationships. Their emotional stability is based on how others react and interact with them. *Oranges* more than any other type are the most concerned with making a good impression. They work hard to gain the appreciation of others. Once *oranges* know they are loved and appreciated, then their emotional anxieties are relieved and their caretaking qualities can shine.

Self-control is not usually a problem for an *orange*. However, when they are experiencing difficulties in their relationships, they have a tendency toward addictions such as eating disorders, and alcohol and substance abuse. *Oranges* struggle deeply with having to cope with problems that are emotional in nature and/or threaten their security. The behavioral pattern for *oranges* in this situation is to create an abundance of petty problems so they will not have to deal with real issues. If they feel that the problem is more than they can emotionally handle, they suffer from depression or become physically ill.

Extroverted Oranges

Extroverted *oranges* are warm, friendly, good-natured, and charming types. They bring humor to situations and enjoy events and activities that encourage laughter and jovial interaction. They tend to view life as an eternal cornucopia from which flows an endless supply of sensual-aesthetic experiences.

Working with an extroverted *orange* is rarely dull.

They are friendly motivators who look for ways to make work more fun even though they work diligently. They add zip to the workplace and are the caretakers of the office social calendar. They will plan Christmas parties, birthday parties, employee farewells, employee-recognition events, and contests. They manage the details of these events with great ease.

Extroverted *oranges* tend to overextend themselves. Since they make handling details and people look so easy and seem to be so skilled at juggling a multitude of tasks, others come to expect this from them. Instead of saying no, an *orange* will just keep on going and doing until they run themselves into the ground. They have a difficult time pacing themselves. They are so driven by the need to be appreciated and considered a valuable part of the team that they forget they can run out of energy. Extroverted *oranges* are binary—either happy or sad. They are either going full speed ahead or are down for the count.

Introverted Oranges

Quiet, friendly, responsible, and conscientious describes an introverted *orange*. They are painstakingly thorough and accurate. They are patient with details and work steadily to get the job done. As with their extroverted counterparts, it is important for them to be part of the team. However, as with the introverted *reds*, they prefer to work alone. They are modest about their organizational skills and abilities and would rather be loyal followers than leaders. If you were to look behind the scenes of every great leader, you would most likely find an introverted *orange* who is seeing that things get done.

Introverted *oranges* do not enter into activities impulsively. Once they do get involved, they are extremely focused and hard to distract. They do not quit easily and will stay committed to the project or tasks at hand until the job is done.

Introverted *oranges* are intensely private people. They find it difficult to express themselves and tend to hold things inside. Actually, all they are doing is observing and listening so they can determine if the person is someone who they want to include in their relationship network. Introverted *oranges* are very selective about whom they choose to share their time, energy, and feelings with.

Reflection

The orange's world is filled with caretaking of family, friends, co-workers, associates, and neighbors— anyone who has a need. Oranges are realistic and down-to-earth people.

Relating to the automobile, the orange would be the body and the windows, sheltering and protecting the occupants, keeping them safe and secure.

Chapter 6

The Yellow Personality

"Yellow is the color of intellect, innovation, and the love for things that are contemporary and challenging."
— Faber Birren

Yellows are self-confident personalities. The "self" words that best describe *yellows* are *self-reliant, self-made, self-respected, self-motivated, self-starting,* and *self-fulfilled. Yellows* believe in themselves, their capabilities, and their intellectual abilities. They know that if they put their minds to it, they can accomplish anything. Their philosophy is that if they can conceive it, they can achieve it. When you add in the *yellow* characteristic of ambition, you realize that they truly are capable of transforming their dreams into real accomplishments. To *yellows*, the future is a world of endless possibilities and the opportunity to make a difference. *Yellows* are true visionaries.

Yellows are natural leaders who instinctively move to the helm. They have a leadership persona that lets others know they are capable of taking charge. Their leadership style is evident in all of their relationships: family, friends, work, and community. However, it is the work environment that provides *yellows* the greatest opportunity to bring their gifts and talents for leadership to their greatest fruition. In fact, *yellows* are most capable of reaching their true potential when they are in charge. They enjoy the challenges that come with taking on the leadership role. They are at ease and confident in assuming enormous responsibilities. Consequently, others are glad to have *yellows* step forward, make the tough decisions, and deal with problems and obstacles. Except for *reds,* most people find it comforting to have someone they can depend on who will be their protector, someone who is willing to stand up and speak out, someone they know they can trust and rely on and see as a competent leader. The relationship between *reds* and *yellows* can be highly competitive because each thinks they should be in the leadership position.

Yellows are challengers. Critical and opinionated, they challenge the way things are done, and they challenge authority. They challenge the traditional ways of thinking, and they challenge why and how things work. They even challenge themselves to be better and to think differently. Their motto is "Think outside of the box." They are conceptual thinkers and see the big picture, so they are not bound by the same mental restrictions or emotional fears that limit other personality types. *Yellows* dare to do things differently and strive to make things better. They are always looking for ways to build a better mousetrap. *Yellows* are nonconformists and are seen as mavericks. For other personality types, *yellows* are often seen as loose cannons, doing what they want without giving thought to how things have been done in the past, or as dreamers who have their heads in the clouds. This is not the case; *yellows* have a very clear vision of where they are going. They just do not always find it necessary to tell others. They are analytical thinkers and are very strategic in their planning. Once they determine the best way that something should be done, then they move forward without distraction.

Yellows struggle throughout their lives trying to conform to the rules of society. They are truly square pegs trying to fit into a round world. *Yellows* live by their own internal code of values and principles. They are not strongly influenced by other people or by traditional limitations. They have their own game plan as to what they think their life should be and what they should accomplish. They are tenacious people and have true grit. *Yellows* are courageous in their thinking and will not back down if they believe something is not right. Their creativity comes from their capacity for deep thinking. They speculate endlessly about the what and why before making their decisions. When bogged down in their thinking, they may suffer from analysis paralysis. *Yellows* enjoy a good debate and will not retreat from a stimulating conversation or a sparring match of words and thoughts. They enjoy the opportunity to change the perspective and thinking of others.

Yellows, like *reds*, are competitive personalities. However, unlike *reds*, where winning is everything, *yellows* will not compete against anyone they think is inferior to them in either thinking or skills. For *reds*, being competitive means winning. In contrast, the kind of competition that stimulates *yellows* is the kind where they are competing against someone they view as a formidable competitor and where the outcome will be meaningful to them. *Yellows* must compete against someone they respect, someone they can learn from, or someone who they view as their peer or competitive superior. *Yellows* will not seek out those who they believe they can readily beat. In these situations, winning is not meaningful. In fact, for *yellows*, competition must fill an ego need. Otherwise, it wastes their time.

Yellows need the freedom to utilize their intelligence, to pursue their quest for knowledge and wisdom, and to develop competency by acquiring new skills and expanding their capabilities. For *yellows*, being competent and a self- acknowl- edged expert is most important. They will not settle for anything less. They pride themselves on their expertise and intellect. They view life as something to be understood and mastered. Research is their forte. They make great researchers because of their need to understand, predict, and explain both concept and reality. They are compulsive about improving things. For *yellows*, knowing how something works is only half the equation. Knowing how to make it better is the other half.

Yellows are idea people who have the capability of turning ideas into reality. For *yellows*, ideas are merely solutions to problems. Instead of dwelling on problems, they focus on solving them. For *yellows*, problems are opportunities to learn, flex their intellectual capabilities, and challenge their skills. They are cerebral people who are multisensory in the way they see things. Their sixth sense is an integral part of their mental functioning. They approach thinking from a logical perspective, trusting and using their five senses to supply the needed information and then crossing over to access their intuitive insights to provide all of the possible scenarios. For *yellows*, exploring concepts, possibilities, and ideas is stimulating. They are happiest when they are being challenged mentally and when they must assimilate and manipulate information. They need to be allowed to have the time to work through the information the way they are mentally programmed. If they do not, they become resentful and unwilling to make decisions.

Yellows are overly critical, authoritarian, and can be arrogant personalities. They are driven by the need for perfection from both themselves and others. To *yellows*, there is only one way to do things and that is *their* way. *Yellows* are the most self-critical of all the personalities. They will badger themselves about their errors in judgment. They are ruthless in monitoring their own progress, and they never need others to point out their shortcomings. They do it themselves. *Yellows* do not need critics; they can be their own worst critic. For *yellows*, to obtain what they perceive as perfection, they are constantly evaluating, analyzing, and escalating their standards. What is accepted by *yellows* as a satisfactory performance one day may only be adequate the next. And, being "just adequate" is viewed as missing the mark. They have very high standards of excellence. Their drive for perfection creates a constant low-level anxiety of self-doubt within themselves. The greatest challenge for *yellows* is to learn how to trust both their logic and their emotions. Trusting emotions is not something they do instinctively or easily. This is not to say that they are not emotionally sensitive people, because they are; they just do not use their emotions to make decisions, nor do they show them readily to others.

Yellows are planners and organizers. They are masters at designing and perfecting systems and procedures to get the best results. If they were going on a trip, they would plan the whole thing out in such detail that they could tell you precisely how long the trip is, what to expect the weather to be, and what clothing to take, anticipating all possible scenarios. They would verify all of the reservations well in advance of departure. They would be able to tell you what activities are available, which geographic sites to visit, and what local events will be happening so you will have a variety of choices to make. *Yellows* need choices; they do not tolerate being boxed in or having someone else telling them what to do. For *yellows*, the preparation for the trip is as much fun as the trip itself. The challenge is to know everything in advance.

Yellows, although athletic, do not like repetitive physical labor. They would rather hire someone else to perform tasks that are repetitious or mundane. In the workplace, *yellows* are known for delegation of tasks that they feel do not fully utilize their capabilities. This is one of the reasons why *yellows* are most often found in leadership positions. They are systems people. They make lists and review those lists many times to ensure that nothing important gets left behind or forgotten. Part of their need to make lists is that their mind is usually so filled with "stuff" that they forget to do what they need to do, such as eating, sleeping, resting, or playing.

At their best, *yellows* are people who can cut through the smokescreens of tradition and focus on the crux of a situation. They have the instinctive insight to be able to see new directions and solutions that will be of the greatest value for all involved. *Yellows* have a keen sense for forecasting and predicting the future, and they are innovative, resourceful thinkers. They can grasp abstract theory easily and convert it into practical applications, and they thrive on complex problems and situations.

Yellows enjoy interaction with people when the conversations are philosophical, intellectual, and non-emotional. They are attracted to people who stimulate their thinking. *Yellows* take criticism very seriously. However, criticism does not intimidate them. If they think they can learn from criticism, they will take it to heart and think about it. On the other hand, if the criticism is viewed as an emotional outburst representing someone else's inability to deal with issues, do not expect *yellows* to sit back and take it. They have an inner sense of rightness and fairness. Do not question their ethics, for they will unleash a strong emotional reaction that is curt, tactless, and often hurtful to others. They can be very aggressive people when their ethics are being challenged. *Yellows* are quick to point out the faults in their attacker's thinking and will openly mount a counterattack. *Yellows* use their intellect as a means of gaining superiority over others.

At their worst, *yellows* are impractical, condescending, overly conceptual, uncompromising, verbose, and nit-picky. They become preoccupied, mentally incapacitated, impatient with others, and irritable. They lose touch with reality and get lost in their heads. Their thinking becomes fuzzy and confused. They get so caught up in trying to rationalize their way of thinking that they lose sight of the objectives. When *yellows* are in this mental state, they tend to intellectualize as a means of not letting others know where they are. They will always take full responsibility for things if appropriate, and if not, they will quickly point out what should be done to correct the situation.

Extroverted Yellows

Extroverted *yellows* are hearty, frank, highly energetic, dynamic, charismatic people. They love to engage people in intellectual banter. They are skilled at persuading others to come over to their way of thinking and support their objectives. They enjoy situations that encourage people to think differently. Extroverted *yellows* are always seeking new challenges. They are the consummate entrepreneurs. If *yellows* are told that something cannot be done but they think it can, they will not only take on the challenge to prove they are right, they will usually exceed expectations. They are masters at fleshing out ideas. They have a natural zest for life and for understanding the complexities of it. They are commandants. They believe it is their place to lead in life and attract people who want to follow their leadership. Their methodology in getting others involved can be likened to the "Tom Sawyer" technique: Make it look easy and so much fun that others cannot possibly resist the temptation to get in and roll up their sleeves to make things happen.

Extroverted *yellows* enjoy public speaking and sharing their thoughts and ideas with people. They understand that in order to be good leaders, they must lead by example. They believe in walking their talk. They know that mixed messages will undermine others' beliefs in them. They are outwardly driven in their thinking, and they need to make things happen. In the game of life, extroverted *yellows* cannot remain on the sidelines. They not only need to be involved in the game, they need to be leading the team.

Introverted Yellows

Introverted *yellows* are the deepest of thinkers. An ideal job for them would be in a "think tank" environment where they would get paid for just thinking. They are constantly creating ideas and concepts and looking for solutions. They have rich imaginations that provide them with endless possibilities to explore. Their thinking process is to consider the possibilities, take action, then reconsider ways to do it better the next time. Introverted *yellows* need the time to think about things, and then think about them some more. They become irritated when pressed to make a decision before they have had the time to fully understand all of the variables. They will probe a problem until they can find the perfect solution. Introverted *yellows* carry on extensive internal mental conversations with themselves. They play out scenario after scenario in their minds and thrive on the complexities of their thoughts. The problem with introverted *yellows* is that most people cannot even comprehend what is going on in their minds. This is because introverted *yellows* do not find it necessary to communicate their thoughts. And, when they do try to explain what they are thinking, it is usually so complicated that others cannot follow them. This adds to their frustration, so they reason, *why try?* It wastes their time and energy.

The faith that introverted *yellows* have in their intuition makes them extremely independent and individualistic. They tend to live by their own intellectual formulas and expect others to fall into line accordingly. They have a real need for autonomy. They are impatient with other people's inability to make decisions, or their emotional outbursts. Introverted *yellows* are cool thinkers under stress, so others will come to them to solve problems when things feel out of control.

For all *yellows*, their greatest gifts are their thinking abilities and their problem-solving skills.

Reflection

The yellow's world is one of seeking the opportunity to solve problems and to make things better. Yellows challenge the status quo because they believe that everything can be improved upon. Typically, yellows do not fit in because they view life so differently.

The automobile metaphor would cast the yellow as the sophisticated, computerized, electronic and fuel injection systems that enable the vehicle to operate. Their contributions are recognized, but no one understands how they work.

Chapter 7

The Green Personality

"Green is the fresh emblem of well-founded hopes."
— Mary Webb, author of *The Spring of Joy*

Greens live in a world of hopes, dreams, and emotions where the intangibles of life are the most important. Their rich imaginations thrive when using their creative abilities—their minds work quickly, bouncing from one thought to another. *Greens* think in metaphors and analogies, painting vivid pictures in

their
minds; *greens* see life
from a holistic perspective that
allows them to see the complete picture. They love creating ideas and exploring
possibilities. Their minds love pondering every
alternative; brainstorming with others feeds their
need to create and to be around people. Since their preferred mental functioning is totally from the right brain,
greens are not bound by the limitations and mental barriers
that restrict most other types. They focus on what things
could be rather than what they are or are intended to be.
Greens create novel applications for existing products, services,
and operations. When you combine a *green's* ability to see the
whole picture with their sensitivity to the feelings and emotions of others, you see that they are capable of creating
opportunities and solutions that meet the needs of everyone
involved. And, their flair for being different adds an excitement and new twist to the mundane.

Greens have such a clear picture of what is going on
that they immediately accept their vision as being real,
whether it is or not. The problem *greens* most often
face is that they trust and act on their visions
and insight so instinctively that they often
neglect to find the facts to support
the conclusions they have
already reached.

Worse yet, *greens* can get so emotionally caught up in their visions that they will distort vital details to support them. For example, if you have ever been around *greens* when they are excited and telling you a story, you will notice that they jump around. They get so caught up in their thoughts and trying to tell others how they feel that they forget to finish sentences. This can leave the listener wondering what they are talking about, who are they talking about, and what the point is. It becomes the job of the listener to fill in the blanks and figure out where the story is going. The result is that others have a difficult time staying with a *green's* thinking or taking what they say seriously.

The greatest gift of *greens* is their highly developed intuition. This gift allows them to sense what others are feeling and read between the lines. They rely on their hunches and insight to get a real feel for what is happening. *Greens* are masters at looking for hidden meanings and reading body language. They intuitively interpret motives and nonverbal cues so they can effectively get a sense of the emotional atmosphere of their environment. *Greens*, like *yellows*, are multisensory personalities. The difference is that *greens* instinctively trust their emotions and intuition, where *yellows* do not. *Greens* are the most productive and creative when reacting to their intuition and feelings, rather than to logic and reality. They are more at ease with what may be, rather than what is, almost to the extent of waiting for events to catch up to their visions.

Greens love to learn about themselves. They are open and receptive to new ideas, especially if they can relate to those ideas. They want to know as much as they can about why they act the way they do and how they can make their relationships better. Since they are so unique in their approach to life, they spend a lot of time searching for information that helps them better understand who they are. They seek ways to better learn how to cope in a world that does not necessarily accept their emotionalism. They value inspiration and self-expression above anything else, and follow their inspirations with the energy of a flash flood. It is their enthusiasm that inspires others to want to be around *them*.

Greens love the experiences that life offers. They are continually looking for new interests and have difficulty staying with things once they lose

interest. A *green's* life resembles a succession of projects impulsively chosen, quickly started, often abandoned, and usually incomplete. *Greens* start out enthusiastically, only to quit upon realizing that structure and repetition are necessary to successfully reach completion or master the necessary skills. A *green* would rather create than do, since they are long on vision and short on action. They look for the fun in life--they enjoy spontaneity and taking things as they happen. They are not great planners; they just believe that everything will happen the way it is supposed to, and trust that whatever comes along will be right.

Greens continually seek to understand what their life's purpose is, the significance of life itself, and also mental, emotional, and spiritual expansion. Their lives are full of events that they see as lessons. Driven to trust and follow their hearts, *greens* are tuned into and sustained by their inner feelings and belief systems. They have an exceptional ability to perceive beauty and wonder in everything around them, both in

people and in nature. They view themselves as unique individuals and renaissance people. *Greens* have an intense need to make their lives count—their lives must have purpose in order for them to feel fulfilled. They believe that they did not come into this life just to take up space, that their life is a self-reflective quest. Always wanting to become their true authentic selves, *greens* can never truly be themselves, since the very act of reaching for self immediately puts it out of reach. This paradox of "one becoming self, if self continues to change" is the burden that *greens* carry throughout their lives. Their endless search for self causes them frustration, guilt, and anxiety. It leaves them believing that their true self is somehow less than it should be.

Greens are driven by idealism and the belief that their purpose in life is to make the world a different and better place. They feel they must influence the quality of life for others. They are the world's greatest cheerleaders, encouraging others to find a better life, and seeking to better understand their true selves. Many motivational and inspirational writers and speakers are *greens*. This personality type is exceptional at using words that inspire, persuade, and motivate. As writers, *greens* understand that the pen is mightier than the sword.

Greens are perpetually curious and always receptive to change. In fact, change is a necessary part of their lives whether it is home, job, mate, lifestyle, or image. Change is their middle name and if their life feels like it is in a rut, then they will change every aspect of it. Unlike other personality types whose natural tendency is to resist change, *greens* welcome the opportunity to experience new things, meet new people, and learn new skills. The risk that *greens* face is that they are so open to anything new or unconventional that they may spend their lives flitting from one thing to another, never staying with one thing long enough to master it. *Greens* have so many talents that it is difficult for them to choose one to focus on. For a *green*, why choose just one thing when you can have it all. It is not uncommon for a *green* to approach midlife wondering why they have not reached their true potential. Part of their frustration results from the fact that they never stay with anything long enough to reap the rewards. *Greens'* lives usually read like a series of short stories with many different scenarios, each one its own adventure.

Of all of the personality types, *greens* are most drawn to and interested in metaphysics, the extrasensory, and the supernatural. It is not unusual to find *greens* involved in some way with the new movements of thinking, for it provides them a forum and setting for their unconventional beliefs; at the same time, it provides them a safe haven where they can pursue their personal quest for spiritual understanding. A new way of thinking allows *greens* to experience things without fear of being viewed as peculiar. It also allows *greens* to develop relationships with people who are of similar inclination. They are attracted to and seek out others who think like they do and who allow them to get in touch with their deepest feelings without being judged.

Greens are warm, sensitive, gentle, emotional people. Their exciting and nurturing energy acts like a magnet when it comes to attracting others. They are masters at subtly engaging the assistance of others by massaging their egos with interesting and sensitive responses. *Greens* openly flatter people and easily express their appreciation. They take great pleasure in pleasing others and making them happy. They tend to develop deep, lasting friendships. When interacting with others, they carefully search for common ground so they can relate. They instinctively create the illusion of providing a safe, emotional, nonjudgmental environment where people can be themselves.

Greens are driven by the need to be liked, and that need is so strong that they are vulnerable to attracting people who are needy or abusive. The potential risk with these relationships is that they drain *greens* emotionally and energetically so they become physically vulnerable. Their need for a relationship drives them so strongly that they feel inadequate without one, so they tend to create relationships that are co-dependent and not healthy for either party. These relationships are usually volatile and may leave both people with deep emotional wounds that never heal. However, it is not uncommon for *greens* to stay in these relationships, because they believe if they just try harder, things might get better. They tend to see relationship failure as their responsibility. *Greens* are so sensitive to the feelings of others that they often take them on as if they were their own, and thus are vulnerable to the emotional manipulation of others who want to dominate them.

Greens are the chameleons of the personality world. These usually gentle, amicable people often surprise others by becoming openly aggressive and hostile when they feel they are being taken advantage of, or are not being appreciated as unique. When a *green* feels put upon or their feelings get hurt, this normally flexible personality

becomes
red. They become rigid,
moody, pensive, and argumentative. This behavioral change throws
other types off because a *green* will sud-
denly impose their wishes on others, telling
them off or openly seeking revenge for perceived
abuses.

Greens, like *oranges*, dislike conflict and will do their
best to avoid it. They are happiest and most productive
in environments that are conflict free. However, since
that is not always possible, *greens* rely on their highly
developed gift of intuition to provide them insight into
the emotional pulse of their environment. Their intuitive
sense acts like a radar system, alerting them to any
potential for conflict. When *greens* are in a conflict situation, they tend to believe that to differ with a person would mean to reject them personally, and
because they cannot face the possibility of being
rejected, they will keep quiet and withdraw.
Greens will also steer clear of conversations that are heavy or have
the potential for conflict.
Instead, they prefer

to involve themselves in discussions that are self-directed or full of intrigue. *Greens* love romance, melodrama, and involvement in interactions that feed their imagination.

Greens are natural champions of the downtrodden, the environment, and human rights. They base their judgments subjectively on human, aesthetic, and civil values. Their interest in their fellow human beings and the environment is genuine. As the humanitarians of the world, they will become relentless when fighting for deeply held beliefs. They will commit whatever it takes to redress social injustice: time, money, or energy. Their dedication to a particular cause is directly tied to the pull it has on their heartstrings.

Extroverted Greens

An extroverted *green's* motto is "Ready-fire-aim." These *greens* are more interested in jumping right in and getting started than they are in figuring out what needs to be done and in what sequence. Consequently, they spend a lot of time having to redo. They rely on their abilities to intuitively know what needs to be done rather than preparing in advance. Extroverted *greens* are high-spirited and have a zest for life that is a combination of enthusiasm, effervescence, and social gregariousness. Their philosophy is to maximize life's options. For these *greens*, life is full of endless possibilities and alternatives and a host of interpersonal encounters just waiting to happen. The problem is that they get so caught up in their current projects or interests that they think of little else.

When the chips are down, you can always count on an extroverted *green* to come through with something positive to say that will inspire. They are experts at rallying the troops together by calling on their sense of creativity, perseverance, and humor. They are witty and clever and tell jokes and stories to lighten things up. They always look for the rainbow even in the darkest of times. They have the capacity to motivate and make others feel that they can accomplish anything, and they tend to take on a fearless persona. They love to be the center of attention and lead others by their enthusiasm.

Extroverted *greens* tend to think out loud and need input and direction. They will openly seek emotional counsel from people when trying to make a decision. Their pattern is such that they will ask someone for their opinion and then will make their decision based on what that person said. The problem begins when they go to another person and ask them for their input and once again change their mind. This changing of one's mind with every person they talk to sends mixed signals. It confuses others and can become a source of frustration to those who work or live with them. Before too long, people start to ask themselves why they should take the time to provide feedback. They know the *green* is just going to change their mind depending on what input has just been received.

Introverted Greens

Introverted *greens* present quite the opposite persona from their extroverted counterparts. They are calm, quiet, reserved, and even shy. They do not like to be the center of attention. In fact, they are more interested in hearing about others than talking about themselves. Although they may demonstrate a cool reserve, they are loving, warm people. They have a capacity for a depth of caring that is not generally found in the other types. However, introverted *greens* are very particular about whom they share their feelings with. They must feel very safe and secure with a person before they will open up.

Unlike extroverted *greens*, introverted *greens* find self-expression difficult. Being reflective, contemplative, meditative, and inwardly focused people, they derive pleasure from interacting with their own active imaginations. Good listeners and sympathetic observers, they love to watch and listen to people and enjoy internalizing what they perceive. Once they get to know you and determine you are someone they like, they are open and enthusiastic.

For these *greens*, a harmonious environment is very important to their emotional well-being. If subjected to hostile, conflict-ridden environments, they internalize their feelings so deeply that they withdraw and find it difficult to deal with the world. Introverted *greens* find that being reclusive is very appealing. For them, life is often so emotionally brutal that they withdraw into their own world just to survive.

Reflection

The green's world is filled with optimism,
dreams, and fantasies. Their role is to create
and to learn. Greens are involved in life and
respond to it with emotion and enthusiasm.

In the automobile, the green would be the
rich leather seats, the eight-speaker
sound system, and the convertible
top—the fun stuff.

Chapter 8

The Role of Personality in Illness

*"Every situation properly perceived becomes
the opportunity to heal."*
— A Course in Miracles

Roxanne was a *green* personality type. She came to see me because she was unable to get pregnant and was concerned, at age 38, that time was running out. She told me that ever since she was a child, she had dreamed of having her own family. At age 32, she finally met Mr. Right. For six years, they had been trying to start their family, to no avail. She had seen many doctors and was told there was nothing physically wrong that would prevent her from having children. This confused and dismayed her. It created a tremendous amount of stress in her relationship and in herself. The reason that she came to me was to see if perhaps I could provide some insight into what could be preventing her from getting pregnant. She was curious to know if there were any blockages energetically, emotionally, or psychologically that were preventing conception. Roxanne's desire to have a child had turned into an obsession. She was frustrated and disappointed with herself. In her words, "I am a mess. My body is a mess and my life is a mess."

It did not take me long to identify stress as one of the primary contributors to her problem—the stress of trying to function as someone other than who she really was. She was a *green* personality trying to live her life as a *red* most of the time. If you go back and read the descriptions of the *green* and *red* personalities, you too will see that the way each of these types thinks and approaches life is very different.

Roxanne was vice president of marketing for a large corporation. Her job responsibilities were very demanding and required her to travel frequently. While she liked parts of her job and the opportunity to meet new people and experience new things, the pace was draining energetically, emotionally, mentally, and physically. Roxanne took the job thinking that it would be creative and allow her to implement many of her ideas, but she found that there was no time for creativity. Responsible for managing details and coordinating the efforts of 16 people, her work required that she deal with deadlines and maintain a very disciplined time schedule. She was always tired, a point that her boss brought to her attention regularly. She was always behind and could never seem to fit everything in. When she finally got home, there never seemed to be time to relax and unwind. Always playing catch-up, she was spreading herself thin—frequently to the point of physical exhaustion.

The stress that was created from her having to function as a different personality color for a prolonged period of time was taking its toll on her health, her relationship, and her life. She felt that her life was difficult and had lost its joy. *Greens* need to have fun and feel free. She was feeling trapped and did not know how to get out of it. She thought if she just tried harder and managed her time better, she could manage it.

As a *green*, Roxanne's weak site was her chest and upper neck area. She suffered regularly from shoulder and neck muscle tension, hyperthyroidism, high blood pressure, frequent coughing, and a shortness of breath. Trying to live her life as a *red* personality whose weak site is the pelvic area, she had developed many typical *red* symptoms. Her hormones were out of balance, and there was a large energy protrusion in her pelvic area, specifically her uterus. What I found was that the hardness that she felt in life had manifested itself into a fibroid cyst in the uterus. There were indicators of endometriosis and a lesion on the right ovary; when I asked if her doctor had discussed these problems with her, she said no. I suggested she go back to her doctor and confirm my findings. Because Roxanne kept telling herself that she was a mess and both her thoughts and emotions supported that belief, she was actually creating that mess inside of her—her emotions were on a roller coaster, her thinking was confused, and her body was chemically out of balance. While all of these factors were significant enough to contribute to her inability to become pregnant, from my perspective the primary factor was that she had been functioning for so long as someone other than whom she really was. The price she was paying was affecting her health.

The first thing I suggested was that she learn more about who she really was. If she better understood herself, her core personality color, and its strengths and weaknesses, then she could learn how to function as another color without it taking so much out of her. I suggested that she begin to embrace the *green* that she was. Not only would she be more productive, but she would also get back her sense of joy and satisfaction from life. Next, I suggested that she find out if the travel could be reduced. While *greens* love new experiences and the

change that travel offers, it is very difficult for them. For *greens*, their home is their sanctuary and the place they go to cocoon and put themselves back together. Without the anchor of home, they get off center. Another suggestion was that she and her husband spend more time together to reestablish the bonds that brought them together in the first place. My final suggestion was that she lighten up on herself, quit trying so hard, and stop being so negative. I encouraged her to listen to her self-talk and specifically stop telling herself that everything was a mess. As long as she kept doing so, she would *continue* to be a mess. Her session strongly validated the premise that our personality and the impact it has on our lives plays a significant role in why we become ill.

I do not always get feedback from my sessions; however, in this case, Roxanne shared that she had gone home and announced to her husband that she was a *green* personality and needed to start living like one again. She explained what a *green* was, and he told her that was

who
he fell in love with, and he
had been concerned because she
had changed so much. They talked about
her job. While he knew how much she liked it,
he was very supportive of less travel. He told her that
he was lonely and missed spending time with his best
friend. They both made the decision that if the travel could
not be reduced, she would seek another position. As it turned
out, a job change was not necessary because her boss had
already planned to talk to her about redefining her job responsibilities and eliminating most of her traveling. Those changes
would also require her to be more creative.

Roxanne went back to her doctor and had her listen to the
part of the audiocassette from her session concerning the
fibroid cyst and endometriosis. The doctor confirmed both and
also found the lesion on the right ovary. Steps were taken to
correct the problems.

Roxanne's mother sat in front of me ten months
after my session with Roxanne. She told me that
Roxanne is a completely different person, back to
her old self, and three months pregnant.
While not all stories have happy end-
ings, the case of Roxanne was
different because

she was willing to do whatever was necessary to get what she wanted. Her story shows that if we are willing to accept who we are and change what is preventing us from fulfilling our desires, anything is possible.

Illness—an Information Source

Illness is our body's way of telling us that something is not working right. It acts as a feedback system alerting us that there is a breakdown in the internal communication network between the body, mind, and spirit. Illness has a purpose—it creates an awareness that the natural rhythmic patterns of the body have been interrupted by some imbalance or malfunction. These imbalances or malfunctions, whether energetic or chemical in nature, inhibit the body's ability to function properly. When illness occurs, we must focus on and listen to what it is telling us so we can restore it back to its proper functioning.

Illness has many meanings, some more obvious than others. When illness occurs in the physical body, it is easy to interpret what it is trying to tell us because of the physical symptoms it creates. Physical symptoms immediately get the attention of the mind and tell it what the body needs. For instance, maybe it needs more sleep, a change in diet, a change in lifestyle, less stress, or more exercise. How do we interpret what that illness is trying to tell us at a deeper level—say, at the level of our energy system? Illness created at this level is our spirit's way of telling us that we have forgotten to recognize the important role it plays in our overall state of health and well-being. It reminds us that the spiritual self is just as important as the physical self. And, if we are to remain healthy and keep the physical body functioning properly, it too needs to be fed, nurtured, and exercised. We cannot neglect our spirit without creating an imbalance or malfunction in all other aspects of who we are: mental, emotional, or physical.

Illness created at the mental level is telling us that we need to change our thoughts, perceptions, and beliefs. Many of the inabilities and hidden blocks associated with illness lie more in our beliefs than in our bodies. Listen to your self-talk and learn to "eavesdrop" on your thoughts. For example, if you are always saying, "I'm confused," it will create confusion in the mind and a sense of not being in control of your life.

"This job is killing me" weakens the immune system. "That person is a real pain in the neck" literally can cre-

ate a pain in the neck. Oh, and how about, "You make me sick." That one really gets us and in fact creates illness throughout the entire body. If your thoughts are negative and self-critical, then they can trigger strong emotional reactions that can manifest what you are thinking. If your thoughts do not promote your feeling good about yourself, then you will not feel good, period.

At an emotional level, illness is telling us how our thoughts are affecting us. Emotions are judgments we create that support our thinking and beliefs. They tell the truth about where we are in life. What I have found in my work with the energy system is that the majority of the illnesses are created within the emotional layer of energy. I have learned that it is the type of emotions people create and how they deal with their emotions that has the most significant impact on their health. When we create emotions that cause a negative reaction such as anger, hatred, hostility, resentment, guilt, or frustration, we create a chemical toxicity in the body that weakens it and increases the potential for illness and infection. Emotions that we do not deal with end up leaving deep hurts and wounds that we often carry throughout our entire lives. When we give power to our emotional hurts, we give away our personal power. I have also learned that while we all share many of the same fears, insecurities, anxieties, and emotional reactions, each of the four different personality types tends to have very specific issues that affect specific areas of the body.

New scientific evidence in the fields of behavioral and energy medicine is supporting the premise that the real cause of illness lies in our thoughts and emotions, and those two factors affect the endocrine system, the chemistry of the body, and the immune system. What researchers are learning about illness is that people who consistently become ill show very specific patterns, including:

1. Viewing life from a negative perspective
2. Inability to deal with their emotions and having unresolved emotional issues that consume their thoughts
3. Unwillingness to change patterns of behavior that are negative and self-destructive
4. Inability to give and receive love
5. Lacking a sense of humor to help relieve the seriousness of life

6. A tendency to deny themselves the things that would improve their quality of life
7. Feeling powerless to make their own choices
8. Inability to remain flexible so they can flow with life's challenges
9. Seeing their life as pointless and having no meaning or purpose
10. Not attending to the needs of their physical body
11. Unwillingness to manage stress

Illness robs us of energy and of life itself. It distorts the messages being sent between the mind and body, and throws every part of us out of sync. Illness involves the whole person, not just specific sites within the body where symptoms are surfacing. When you look at illness and what causes it, look at it from all aspects of your life. Consider your lifestyle, your relationships with others, your relationship with yourself, what creates stress in your life, your fears, your personality type, and the habits you create as a result of your personality type. Dr. Bernie Siegel, author and inspirational speaker, reminds us that there are no incurable illnesses, only incurable people.

Personality and Illness

There is a direct correlation between the genetic aspect of our personality and illness. That aspect directs the way our mind communicates with our physical body and the habits we create. When it comes to our health, how we think and react directly affects the balance and well-being of our body. Since personality is something that is instinctive, we tend to take it for granted. We forget to pay attention to the habits and the comfort zones we create as a result of it. While these habits and comfort zones help us function effectively in one aspect of our life, they may in fact inhibit and even sabotage another aspect of our life, such as our health.

Let me show you what I mean. Personalities who are *reds* and *oranges* are well equipped to deal with reality and basic survival needs because of their personality strengths and their approach to life. Yet, in order to help themselves cope, they tend to create habits such as smoking, drinking, and taking medications to help them relax. These personalities are usually so busy living, working, and taking care of the basic human needs of others that they forget to take time to care for themselves. They are so intense in their focus that they tend to stay tense for longer periods of time, and consequently suffer from lower back pain, and aches and pains in the muscles and joints. When I ask them about their health habits, it is not uncommon to hear them say that they are too busy to find the time to put something together on a routine basis. When I ask them about getting sick, I have had many *reds* and *oranges* tell me that they do not have time to get sick, so their bodies had better cooperate and learn how to take care of themselves.

Now, let's look at each one of the personality colors and the effect they may have on health. As we cover each of the four colors, I will identify some of the most common emotional and psychological issues that each color struggles with; where their weak sites are in the body; which glands, organs and major systems of the body are affected; and list some of the potential types of illness each personality has a predisposition for developing.

Before we begin the process of self-exploration, let me first define what I mean by "weak site." In the energy system, the weak site is where the root cause of illness originates. The energetic information contained within the weak site identifies if the illness was created within the emotional or mental layer of energy. It points out the severity of the chemical change in the body and which other parts of the body will be affected.

In the physical body, the weak site is the most vulnerable part of the body that has the greatest susceptibility to imbalance, illness, and malfunction. It is where most symptoms of illness will first surface. Take a moment and think about your health and which areas in your body are the source of the greatest problems. Now, go back and look at your childhood health issues. You will probably find that the majority of your illnesses always tended to be in one area of your body. Perhaps you suffered more from respiratory problems or digestive problems or structural and skeletal problems or problems with elimination. Each one of these health issues is directly connected to specific weak sites in the body.

With respect to personality, the weak site contains information that identifies how a person mentally functions and relates to their external world. It reveals what kinds of emotional and psychological issues the person consistently struggles with. It identifies the predictable behavioral patterns that determine the person's approach to life and how they deal with the challenges that life offers them.

Behavioral Patterns and Weak Site of the Red Personality

Reds work too hard and are continually pushing themselves, often to the point of physical exhaustion. They are prime candidates for health issues because of the way they deal with stress. They are excitable personalities who anger easily, and they become vocal and physically aggressive when feeling threatened. Their eating habits are such that it is not uncommon for them to miss meals, eat only one meal a day, or grab something quick just to satisfy their hunger. They tend to have difficulty relaxing or getting a good night's sleep. When they're tired, *reds* become emotionally overwhelmed, sometimes to the point of being distraught. In this mental state, they cannot think clearly or cope with anything. They become repetitious in what they say, somehow thinking that repetition will help them achieve clarity of thought. They will create multiple problems so they can avoid having to deal with real issues. Their insecurities arise when they feel "unsafe" in their environment. *Reds* tend to display obsessive-compulsive behavioral patterns, especially when feeling out of control. Some of the emotional and psychological anxieties and insecurities that *reds* display are:

1. Fear of not being able to provide basic human necessities
2. Fear of being emotionally vulnerable
3. Fear of poverty
4. Fear of being powerless
5. Paranoia around personal safety and security
6. Fear of loss of personal possessions and financial assets
7. Fear of other people taking advantage of them financially
8. Fear of personal intimacy
9. Anxieties that they cannot make things happen the way they need them to in order to feel some measure of success
10. Frustration around not being able to control people and their environment
11. Fear of being out of control
12. Feeling sorry for self
13. Avoidance of emotional needs and deep feelings
14. Exaggerating the truth in order to make others think they are in control or important
15. Sexual anxieties

Weak site: A red's weak site is in the pelvic area, legs, feet, and entire spinal column. The systems affected are the immune system, digestive system, and circulatory system. The glands and organs affected are the reproductive organs, adrenals, spleen, and heart.

Potential health issues: Hypertension, heart disease, stroke, hyperthyroidism, chronic lower back pain, sciatica, bowel and rectal disorders, pelvic hip and joint disorders, tumor and cancer of pelvic area, pelvic inflammatory diseases, prostate cancer, leg cramps, circulation problems in legs and feet, phlebitis, varicose veins, ulcers, anxiety attacks, chronic stress syndrome, alcohol abuse, indigestion, diarrhea, impotency, urinary infections, osteoarthritis, blood ailments, and insomnia.

Behavioral Patterns and Weak Site of the Orange Personality

Oranges are worriers. They continually live with a low level of anxiety about life. They tend to take on too much and let other people's problems become their own. They strive too hard to fulfill the needs of others. They struggle with the conflict between the responsibilities of family and work. *Oranges* need familiarity and security and become anxious when either are in jeopardy. When stressed, they become erratic and suffer from emotional outbursts and deep states of depression. Their outlook on life becomes negative, and life itself becomes hard. When depressed, they use food as a means of emotional comfort, and they tend to struggle with weight issues. This personality type has a predisposition toward addictions: alcohol, substance abuse, gambling, and compulsive spending. They are passive-aggressive in their behavior and have a tendency to hold in their emotions until they reach a boiling point; then they let loose and immediately feel guilty for doing so. Some of the emotional and psychological anxieties and insecurities displayed by *oranges* are:

1. Fear of abandonment
2. Fear of being unsupported by others; of being alone
3. Anxieties around never having enough
4. Fear of being taken advantage of, being manipulated and controlled

5. Feelings of guilt and resentment toward others when not appreciated
6. Fear of loss of job or family
7. Feelings of being victimized by one's circumstances, sexual preferences, or ethnic origin
8. Inability to take responsibility for their lives
9. Feeling powerless to make their own choices
10. Denying themselves what they need to maintain their quality of life
11. Fear of not being able to take care of themselves financially
12. Frustrations around sexuality and sexual performance
13. Feelings of resentment over others having control over them
14. Fear of the unknown
15. Feelings of guilt around not being an adequate partner in their relationship

Weak site: An *orange's* weak site is the lower abdomen and lower back (specifically lumbar and sacral spinal area). The areas affected are the reproductive, respiratory, circulatory, and muscle systems. The glands and organs affected are the pancreas, reproductive organs (ovaries and testes), thyroid, small and large intestine, bladder, and kidneys.

Potential health issues: Men: prostate, hormone imbalance, impotency, testicular cancer. Women: menstrual difficulties, vaginitis, fibroid cysts and tumors in uterus, ovarian cysts, endometriosis, hormone imbalances, and breast, cervical, uterine, and ovarian cancer. Fibromyalgia, rheumatoid arthritis, diabetes, manic depression, candidiasis, chronic mid- and lower-back pain, disk problems (ruptured or slipped disks), chronic fatigue syndrome, pancreatitis, pancreatic cancer, kidney disease, urinary infections, kidney stones, mental exhaustion, and constipation.

Behavioral Patterns and Weak Site of the Yellow Personality

Yellows are perfectionists; they expect perfection from themselves and everyone else. They constantly push themselves by escalating their personal standards of excellence. They are extremely critical and judgmental of themselves and others. They have a deep inner fear of failure. They have issues around trust and are naturally suspicious of people and what their real motives are. Their work is their life, so they tend to become singularly focused, leaving little time for relaxation or for other people. Their frustration involves people who are illogical and who display emotional outbursts. They are resentful of those who push them to make decisions before they are ready. When stressed, *yellows* get nit-picky and argumentative. They become indignant when accused of doing something that is not honest or ethical; their behavior

instantly changes and they become aggressive and show open hostility. Their analytical nature creates constant conflict between what their head thinks and their heart feels. When caught in this thinking dilemma, they experience despair, confusion, and self-doubt; they become immobilized. They lose their confidence and withdraw deeper into themselves, which leaves others wondering what is wrong. *Yellows* do not share their emotions, so others do not know how to help them. They become antisocial. The truth is that when in this state of mind, *yellows* do not want help. They need to work things out themselves. Some of the emotional and psychological anxieties and insecurities displayed by *yellows* are:

1. Fear of rejection and criticism
2. Fear of intimidation
3. Fear of failure
4. Frustration resulting from being pushed by others and told what to do
5. Worrying about having to be accountable to others
6. Anger and resentment resulting from having their integrity questioned
7. Frustration over relationships that are emotionally complex

8. Feeling entrapped in a needy relationship
9. Fear of accepting responsibility for themselves and their commitments
10. Fear of loss of independence and autonomy
11. Resentment over having to take responsibility for others who are incapable of taking care of themselves
12. Self-deception
13. Lack of faith in themselves
14. Fear of looking stupid or incompetent
15. Inability to express and show emotions

Weak site: A *yellow's* weak site is the solar plexus and midback (specifically the thoracic section of the spine). The areas affected are the digestive, immune, central nervous, and skeletal systems. The glands and organs affected are the pituitary and adrenal glands, skin, stomach, liver, gall bladder, spleen, and lower esophagus.

Potential health issues: Chronic digestive disorders, gastritis, stomach cancer, liver disorders, liver cancer, gallstones, ulcers, spastic colon, colitis, autoimmune diseases, lupus, hiatal hernia, chronic stress syndrome, multiple sclerosis, ALS (Lou Gehrig's disease), skin disorders, allergies, herpes simplex virus, herpes zoster virus, arthritis, tendinitis, anemia, mononucleosis, headaches, paralysis, and adrenal dysfunction.

Behavioral Patterns and Weak Site of the Green Personality

Greens suppress their feelings. They will avoid conflict even at their own expense. They blame themselves and continually feel guilty for everything that happens. They accept responsibility for others' faults and see those faults as their own. They are afraid to say no for fear of hurting someone's feelings. They struggle with the feeling that they are not worthy of being loved. How they feel about themselves is directly tied to what is happening in their relationships. For them, life without love is frightening.

Greens tend to involve themselves in relationships

that are emotionally needy, abusive, or not fulfilling. Rejection is devastating emotionally. They wear their hearts on their sleeves for all to see and take advantage of. They can get so caught up in their emotionalism that they lose all objectivity in coping with the real world. They struggle with the inner turmoil of trying to find themselves and how they fit into this world. They tend to feel sorry for themselves and wallow in self-condemnation. When neglected, they become bitter, insensitive, and even cruel. They project dependent-submissive behavioral patterns toward others. Some of the emotional and psychological anxieties and insecurities displayed by *greens* are:

1. Fear that others will use their vulnerabilities against them
2. Frustration with respect to being responsible for the feelings of others
3. Fear of not being loved
4. Confusion around love and what it means
5. Fickleness toward others
6. Jealousy
7. Resentment from holding on to past hurts and emotional abusiveness

8. Depression associated with lack of self-love
9. Harboring negative feelings toward others
10. Self-destructive behavior that perpetuates feelings of inadequacy
11. Fear of being alone
12. Feelings used as an escape or to deny responsibility for their actions
13. Creating co-dependent relationships
14. Tending to stay in relationships that are personally destructive
15. Frustration over the inability to step up to issues and make decisions

Weak site: A *green's* weak site is the chest, shoulders, upper back (cervical spinal area), and neck. The areas affected are the circulatory, respiratory, immune, cerebrospinal, and muscle systems. The glands and organs affected are the thyroid, thymus, pituitary, pineal, lungs, heart, and pancreas.

Potential health issues: Upper neck and muscle tension, migraine headaches, diabetes, thyroid disorders, hypo/hyperglycemia, breast cancer, heart disease, mitral valve prolapse, asthma, chronic respiratory disorder, depression, eating disorders (anorexia and bulimia), hormone imbalances, tinnitus, epilepsy, muscular dystrophy, attention deficit disorder, neurological disorders, bone cancer, allergies, laryngitis, and nervous disorders.

Healing Happens When We Help It

While research is still in the discovery stages with respect to understanding how thoughts and emotions actually relate to the brain's release of chemicals, what has been discovered is that the personality has a direct impact on the creation of thoughts, emotional reactions, and the health of the body. What we now know is that our state of mind directly affects the chemistry of the body in such a way that we are either becoming ill or overcoming illness every moment of our lives. The human body is an extraordinary mechanism that has an astonishing and irrepressible need to stay healthy. It is constantly repairing, renewing, and regenerating itself. Our job is to help it succeed. We can do this by better understanding ourselves, changing our habits, altering our thinking, making corrections on our "path" and eliminating from our lives what is preventing us from staying healthy.

Reflection

Personality ties behavioral and emotional responses to the body.
The body responds by creating weak sites predictable by personality color.

Prepared with the knowledge and understanding of our personality colors, we have an increased awareness of the vulnerability of our state of wellness.

About the Author

Carol Ritberger, Ph.D., medical intuitive, is an innovative leader in the fields of personality typology and intuitive medicine. She has devoted more than 25 years to researching the impact of stress, emotions, and personality type on the health and well-being of the physical body. Carol holds two doctorates, one in religious philosophy and the other in esoteric philosophy and hermetic sciences. Her works include *Your Personality, Your Health* and *Love . . . What's Personality Got to Do with It?* which have received national recognition for their innovative approach to self-help. She has been featured in *Good Housekeeping, Yoga Journal, Woman's World, Men's Health, GQ,* and *Healthy Living;* and has appeared on television programs such as *Extra, Healthy Living,* and *New Attitudes*—as well as on many national radio shows.

Carol is the executive director of The Ritberger Institute, which offers personal and professional development programs. Its goal is to assist its students in accessing and developing their intuition for business, personal, and spiritual growth. It offers an array of classes, including personality training and certification and intuitive-medicine programs.

Carol lives in Northern California with her husband, Bruce, with whom she cofounded The Ritberger Institute. For more information on programs and presentations offered through the institute, please visit her Website: **www.ritberger.com**.

Hay House Titles of Related Interest

YOU CAN HEAL YOUR LIFE, *the movie,*
starring Louise L. Hay & Friends
(available as a 1-DVD program
and an expanded 2-DVD set)
Watch the trailer at: **www.LouiseHayMovie.com**

THE SHIFT, *the movie,*
starring Dr. Wayne W. Dyer
(available as a 1-DVD program
and an expanded 2-DVD set)
Watch the trailer at: **www.DyerMovie.com**

Books

Aromatherapy A–Z, by Connie Higley, Alan Higley,
and Pat Leatham

Colors & Numbers, by Louise L. Hay

Dream Journal, by Leon Nacson

Healing with Herbs and Home Remedies A–Z,
    by Hanna Kroeger

Heal Your Body A–Z, by Louise L. Hay

Home Design with Feng Shui A–Z,
    by Terah Kathryn Collins

Homeopathy A–Z, by Dana Ullman, M.P.H.

Notes

<u>Notes</u>

<u>Notes</u>

<u>Notes</u>

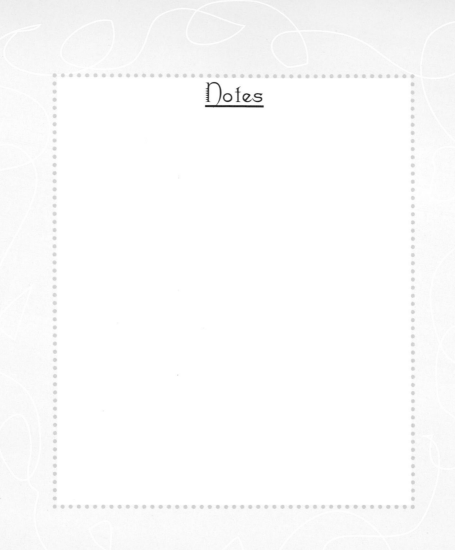

Notes